THE SECOND BLOOM

Reinventing Your Life After Retirement.

NICCI BROCHARD
&
DR. BEN CHUBA

THE SECOND BLOOM

Reinventing Your Life After Retirement.

CROSSBORDER

New York, London, Quebec

CONTENTS

Introduction 1

Chapter 1: The End is Just the Beginning 4

Chapter 2: Who Am I Now? —Rediscovering Identity After Career Life 10

Chapter 3: The Purpose Reboot—Finding Meaning in the Next Chapter 16

Chapter 4: Designing Your Second Act Vision Board 23

Chapter 5: The Power of Passion Projects and Hobbies 30

Chapter 6: Entrepreneurship After 55—Yes, You Can 37

Chapter 7: Lifelong Learning—Brains Don't Expire 44

Chapter 8: Mind & Mood—Emotional Wellness in the Golden Years 52

Chapter 9: Friendships, Sisterhood & Building New Circles 60

Chapter 10: Love, Sex, and Dating After Retirement 67

Chapter 11: Health is Wealth—Moving, Eating, and Thriving .. 74

Chapter 12: Downsizing, Relocating, or Nesting In 82

Chapter 13: Giving Back—Volunteering and Legacy Work 89

Chapter 14: Tech-Savvy, Fear-Free—Embracing the Digital World 96

Chapter 15: Living Boldly—Writing Your Next Chapter with Confidence 105

Conclusion: Living Boldly – The Next Chapter Begins 112

INTRODUCTION

The Second Bloom – Reinventing Your Life After Retirement

Retirement is often viewed as the end of a chapter—a moment when the daily grind of work finally gives way to leisure, relaxation, and perhaps even a well-deserved rest. For many, the idea of retirement is synonymous with freedom from deadlines, commutes, and stress. But for others, it can feel like an uncertain, daunting step into the unknown. As we transition into this new phase of life, it's not uncommon to face a series of questions: What's next? How do I stay fulfilled without the structure of a 9-to-5 job? How do I redefine myself after spending decades wrapped up in a single career?

The truth is, retirement doesn't have to be the end—it can be the beginning of a second bloom. It's an opportunity to reinvent yourself, explore new passions, discover hidden talents, and live with purpose in ways you never could while caught up in the daily demands of work. Far from being a time to "slow down," retirement can be a time to reignite your spirit, reclaim your time, and rediscover joy in everyday living.

As we enter retirement, many of us face the challenge of creating a new identity beyond the professional roles we've played for much of our lives. Our careers have often shaped how we see ourselves, and with the sudden absence of that structure, it's easy to feel lost or disconnected. Yet, the end of a career marks the beginning of an exciting journey. This book, The Second Bloom, is a guide to navigating that journey and embracing the fullness of life after retirement.

This second act can be more than just about filling time. It's about reclaiming your passion, nurturing your mental and physical well-being, and crafting a lifestyle that allows you to live more authentically. Whether you dream of traveling the world, learning new skills, or giving back to your community, this period of life offers unlimited possibilities. The key to making the most of it lies in redefining what success means and learning how to cultivate purpose and joy in new and creative ways.

While the prospect of reinvention may seem overwhelming at first, the truth is that many retirees have already discovered a fulfilling post-career life. The experience gained over the years — through work, relationships, and personal growth—can be harnessed to create something deeply meaningful in your later years. Whether you've spent your career building a business, raising a family, or honing a craft, you have accumulated a wealth of knowledge, wisdom, and experience. This is your chance to share that wealth with others, explore new opportunities, and pursue the dreams that might have been put on hold for years.

In The Second Bloom, we'll explore ways to transform this next phase of life into one that is rich with growth, purpose, and fulfillment. We'll talk about rediscovering old passions and embracing new ones, whether that means picking up a paintbrush, starting a new business, volunteering, or simply deepening your relationships. This book will also address the importance of maintaining mental and physical health, navigating financial adjustments, and finding the emotional strength to adapt to changes in lifestyle, routine, and identity.

For some, the idea of reinvention after retirement may feel like an intimidating challenge. But reinvention is not about drastically changing who you are—it's about tapping into the most vibrant parts of yourself that may have been buried beneath the weight of responsibilities and routines. It's about reconnecting with the things that bring you joy, passion, and a sense of accomplishment, but on your own terms.

As you embark on this journey, remember that retirement is not a destination—it's a new beginning, a chance for growth and a fresh start. You are entering the time of your life when you have the freedom to prioritize what matters most to you. Embrace the opportunity to bloom once again. Your second act can be just as meaningful, vibrant, and full of potential as your first. The only question now is: What will you do with it?

This book will guide you through the process of reimagining retirement and turning it into an exciting new chapter. Together, we'll explore how you can embrace this next stage with confidence, creativity, and a deep sense of purpose. Let's begin this journey of reinvention together and discover the limitless possibilities that await in your second bloom.

CHAPTER 1

THE END IS JUST THE BEGINNING

⌛

Redefining What Retirement Really Means

For many, the word "retirement" conjures up images of endings—the end of a career, the end of daily work routines, and the end of professional identity. It's often perceived as a time to wind down, to slow down, and to let go of the ambition that defined earlier years. However, as we move further into this new era of life, we realize that retirement doesn't have to be a final chapter—it can be the beginning of an entirely new story.

Retirement, in this sense, becomes an opportunity for reinvention, rediscovery, and reclamation. It is a period where, instead of slowing down, we can accelerate the pursuit of passions and activities that bring us joy, fulfillment, and purpose. Many retirees find that this stage of life is the first time they have the freedom to truly explore who they are and what they want, outside the constraints of a job, family obligations, or societal expectations.

Reframing retirement as a new beginning requires a shift in mindset. Rather than focusing on what is being left behind, it's essential to embrace the idea of what comes next—to view retirement as an opening, not a closing. It's a time to ask yourself, "What do I truly want to accomplish now? What dreams have I put on hold that I can finally pursue?" The possibilities are limitless once you redefine what retirement means for you.

For example, take the case of John, a 65-year-old who spent most of his career in corporate management. After retiring, he initially struggled with the transition, feeling disconnected from his former self. Instead of resigning himself to a life of leisure or stagnation, he chose to redefine retirement. John began taking woodworking classes, something he had always been passionate about but never had time for. Over time, he started creating furniture pieces and even began selling them online, bringing in a new sense of accomplishment and fulfillment. For John, retirement wasn't about slowing down—it was about discovering a new passion and channeling his energy into something meaningful.

Debunking Myths About Aging and "Slowing Down"

There are numerous myths surrounding aging and retirement that contribute to a limited and often negative view of this phase of life. Society often portrays aging as a time of inevitable decline, with the expectation that older adults will slow down, retire from active life, and gradually withdraw from social engagements. These stereotypes do not serve anyone, especially when we look at the reality of how many men and women are thriving well into their later years.

- The Myth of Physical Decline: One of the most persistent myths is that physical vitality fades quickly after retirement. While it's true that aging comes with its challenges, such as changes in metabolism, energy levels, and health concerns, many people in their 60s, 70s, and beyond are leading active, healthy lives. Research has shown that staying physically active—through walking, weightlifting, yoga, or cycling—can have profound benefits, slowing the aging process and increasing life expectancy. For example, Jane, a 72-year-old retiree, took up cycling in her 60s and has since completed several cross-country bike trips. Rather than slowing down, she found that staying active helped her manage her health, improve her mental clarity, and maintain a strong social life.

- The Myth of Mental Decline: Another stereotype is that mental sharpness decreases as people age. In reality, retirement can provide an opportunity to exercise the mind in new ways. Many retirees embark on lifelong learning, engaging in activities such as learning new languages, taking up new hobbies, or even going back to school. Studies show that intellectual stimulation can help maintain cognitive health, keeping the mind agile. Consider Alan, a 68-year-old former lawyer who decided to pursue a degree in history after retiring. He found that the challenge of studying complex topics and engaging in academic discourse helped keep his mind sharp and expanded his sense of purpose.

- The Myth of Isolation and Withdrawal: The conventional belief that aging leads to social withdrawal and isolation is equally inaccurate. In fact, retirement offers an opportunity for people to form new social connections, participate in community activities, and create a broader social network. For instance, Emily, a retiree in her early 60s, joined a local community center where she became involved in volunteering and joined several hobbyist groups. Through these activities, she developed deep, meaningful friendships that enriched her life far more than her work environment ever did.

By challenging these myths, we allow ourselves the freedom to embrace retirement not as a time to fade away, but as a time to thrive, expand, and grow in ways that are personally fulfilling and meaningful.

Embracing This Transition as a Personal Renaissance

Retirement can be seen as a personal renaissance, a rebirth of sorts, where all of the accumulated experiences, wisdom, and desires that were previously put on the back burner are now given the chance to flourish. This stage of life is an opportunity for self-discovery, reinvention, and new beginnings.

- A Time for Reinvention: For many, midlife and retirement are times when they can finally step away from the roles they've played for years—whether as professionals, parents, or caretakers—and reimagine their lives. The skills, talents, and insights that were developed in earlier years can now be directed toward new ventures, hobbies, or goals that were once out of reach. This could mean taking up painting, writing, traveling, or launching a small business. Michael, a 55-year-old former corporate executive, took early retirement and used the time to finally start his dream of opening a small café. His years of leadership and management skills made his transition into entrepreneurship seamless, and his new venture brought him both financial success and personal satisfaction.

- Rediscovering Lost Passions: For many, retirement is a time to rekindle old hobbies and interests that were sidelined by career demands and family responsibilities. This could be as simple as rediscovering a love for painting or as profound as learning an entirely new craft or skill. It's a time to reconnect with what truly brings joy and satisfaction. Lori, who spent most of her career as an accountant, rediscovered her passion for photography in retirement. She began taking classes and eventually turned her hobby into a profitable venture, becoming an in-demand portrait photographer in her community.

- Living with Purpose: A personal renaissance in retirement is about finding a renewed sense of purpose and creating a life that is in alignment with one's core values. As work and career no longer define you, you have the opportunity to engage with life in ways that feel genuine and meaningful. For Joseph, a 63-year-old retiree, purpose was found in mentoring young adults. He spent part of his retirement volunteering as a mentor in a local program, helping young men navigate the challenges of adulthood. The sense of fulfillment Joseph derived from giving back became his new purpose, and it allowed him to continue making a positive impact on the world.

Retirement can thus be a profound period of growth, where you transition from merely existing to fully engaging with life. Embracing this transition as a personal renaissance requires shedding the preconceived notions of retirement as a time of slowing down and instead recognizing it as an opportunity to accelerate your life's possibilities.

Conclusion

The first chapter of The Second Bloom introduces the essential concept that retirement is not a final chapter but rather an opportunity for a new beginning—a time to embrace personal growth, reinvention, and rediscovery. It is a period where freedom from the constraints of work and career offers the chance to live with intention and purpose.

By debunking the myths surrounding aging, men and women over 40 can reframe retirement as a time to thrive rather than withdraw. It's a time to pursue old passions, try new things, and discover what truly brings joy and fulfillment. This chapter serves as a call to redefine retirement as a personal renaissance, where emotional, intellectual, and physical growth are not just encouraged but celebrated. Retirement is not the end of a journey but the beginning of something extraordinary—a second bloom.

As you continue this journey, remember that retirement is not a time of slowing down, but rather an exciting new beginning filled with endless opportunities for growth, creativity, and connection.

CHAPTER 2

WHO AM I NOW? —REDISCOVERING IDENTITY AFTER CAREER LIFE

—◦◦❧◦◦—

Introduction: Navigating Life Beyond the Title

For much of our adult lives, we define ourselves by the roles we play. These roles are often tied to our careers—whether as an executive, entrepreneur, doctor, teacher, or other professional identity. Our sense of self-worth and purpose becomes deeply intertwined with our professional success, status, and the work we do every day. Retirement can be a jarring transition, shaking the very foundation of how we see ourselves.

As we step into this new phase of life, the question inevitably arises: Who am I now? Without the career title, the workday routines, and the constant demands of professional life, many retirees experience a crisis of identity. The shift from being a professional to being retired isn't just about leaving work behind—it's about facing the reality that much of who we were has been wrapped up in our roles. This chapter is about rediscovering who you are beyond the title, reimagining your identity, and finding a sense of purpose in a life that may have been largely defined by your career.

1. Letting Go of Titles and Roles

The Power of Professional Titles

For decades, many men and women have tied their identity to their work. Titles such as CEO, doctor, engineer, or lawyer serve not only as professional designations but as markers of value and worth. These roles dictate the way others see us, but they also influence how we perceive ourselves. When the workday ends and retirement begins, these familiar titles no longer define us. This shift can be challenging, particularly when our sense of purpose was deeply intertwined with professional identity.

Letting go of a professional title requires a shift in perspective. It's essential to recognize that while your career has been a significant part of your life, it doesn't define you as a whole person. Your worth is not tied to your role or your ability to produce. In retirement, you have the freedom to explore and redefine your identity in ways that align with your values, interests, and desires.

Letting Go of the Old Self

The first step in this journey of rediscovery is to let go of the old self. This doesn't mean erasing the past or dismissing the hard work you've put into your career—it means acknowledging that who you are is much more than the title or the role you've held. Transitioning from career life to retirement can feel like shedding a skin, but it's an important part of the process of growth and reinvention. This phase invites you to redefine yourself in a way that aligns more closely with who you truly are—without the weight of societal expectations and professional labels.

2. Self-Reflection Exercises to Rediscover Passions and Strengths

Exploring Your Inner Self

Once you let go of the professional title, the next step is to ask yourself: What are the things that truly light me up? What am I passionate about? Retirement is a rare opportunity to rediscover your passions and strengths outside the confines of a career. In this section, we'll explore several self-reflection exercises to help you uncover your authentic self.

Exercise 1: Life Timeline Reflection

Create a timeline of your life, noting significant events, milestones, and achievements from childhood to your professional career. Reflect on the following questions:

- What moments brought you the most joy?
- Which accomplishments are you most proud of?
- Were there passions or hobbies you gave up for your career?

By revisiting your past, you can gain valuable insight into the things that have always brought you fulfillment and meaning, whether that be artistic endeavors, community involvement, or other interests. This timeline helps you reconnect with your **core values** and discover what you still want to pursue.

Exercise 2: The "Why" Exploration

Ask yourself why you chose your career in the first place. What drove you to that path? Was it passion? Financial stability? Status? Once you have this clarity, think about how you can bring elements of that passion into your post-retirement life. For example, if your work was driven by a desire to help people, perhaps you could explore volunteer opportunities in healthcare or mentorship. This exercise will help you identify what drives you, allowing you to reconnect with your sense of purpose in retirement.

Exercise 3: Strengths Inventory

Make a list of your skills and strengths. Include things you learned during your career, but also list personal qualities that might have gone underappreciated—such as resilience, problem-solving, or communication skills. Once you've identified these strengths, think about how they can be applied to new ventures, hobbies, or volunteer opportunities. Many retirees find that their professional skills translate well into new activities, from writing and teaching to starting small businesses or getting involved in local charities.

Real-life Example:

- Patricia, a 62-year-old retired schoolteacher, had spent 35 years teaching high school English. When she retired, she felt a sense of loss without her classroom and students. But through self-reflection exercises, she remembered how much she loved writing poetry and reading books in her spare time. She began attending local writing workshops, eventually publishing a collection of poetry. Patricia's journey of self-discovery and reinvention allowed her to rediscover her passion for writing and find fulfillment in a way that was meaningful for her.

3. The Emotional Impact of Retirement on Self-Worth

The Emotional Adjustment to Retirement

While retirement is often seen as the end of a career, it can also trigger a period of emotional adjustment. The loss of routine, the loss of professional identity, and the shift from an active work life to a more flexible lifestyle can cause feelings of uncertainty, anxiety, and even depression. For many, this emotional upheaval stems from self-worth being too closely tied to one's career. It's important to recognize that retirement presents an opportunity to develop a more balanced and holistic sense of self-worth.

Dealing with Loss of Identity

For men and women who have been working for decades, the transition to retirement can feel like a loss of purpose. It can be a shock to the system when the workday ends and there is no longer a set schedule or clear role. This is often compounded by the societal expectation that people should continue to stay "busy" and "productive" in retirement.

The challenge is to let go of external definitions of success and create a more internalized and sustainable sense of worth. Understanding that value isn't defined by what you do, but who you are, is essential for creating a healthy emotional relationship with retirement. This requires making the shift from doing to being—focusing on the internal qualities that make you a valuable person: your character, your values, and your relationships.

Rebuilding Self-Worth After Retirement

To rebuild a sense of self-worth after retirement, it's important to actively engage in activities that bring joy and fulfillment, whether that means pursuing hobbies, volunteering, or reconnecting with loved ones. Engaging in new challenges, learning opportunities, and creative endeavors helps men and women find a new sense of purpose and self-validation.

For example, James, a 60-year-old retiree, initially felt a sense of loss after retiring from his position as a manager in a logistics company. However, he began volunteering at a local community center, teaching financial literacy to young adults. This gave him a sense of purpose and allowed him to see the direct impact of his knowledge on others. Over time, James built a new sense of self-worth—not from a job title, but from the difference he was making in his community.

Conclusion: Reinventing Yourself in Retirement

The transition to retirement can be daunting, but it also provides an exciting opportunity for self-discovery and reinvention. By letting go of the professional title, engaging in self-reflection, and rebuilding a sense of self-worth, retirement can become a time of personal growth, fulfillment, and purpose. This chapter has explored the emotional complexities of retirement, and the tools and exercises outlined here can help guide you toward a more meaningful and balanced second act.

You are more than your career. Your worth is not determined by your title, your position, or your productivity. By taking the time to rediscover your passions, reconnect with your strengths, and embrace your new identity, you can approach retirement with a sense of excitement, possibility, and renewal. The second bloom is yours for the taking—a time to rewrite your story and live with purpose in a way that aligns with who you are and who you want to become.

CHAPTER 3

THE PURPOSE REBOOT—FINDING MEANING IN THE NEXT CHAPTER

⚜

Introduction: The Quest for Meaning Beyond Career

As we age and transition through major life changes, especially after the age of 55, we often begin to reflect on the purpose that has guided us for much of our lives. For many, career success has been the core of their identity, giving them a sense of direction and significance. But as we reach retirement age or begin to shift focus from career to personal interests, the question inevitably arises: What now? What is my purpose beyond the professional world?

The idea of purpose is not just an abstract concept—it's the fuel that drives us, motivates us, and gives us a sense of meaning. Research has shown that having a strong sense of purpose can contribute to better mental health, physical well-being, and even increased life expectancy. However, many people struggle with this question when they no longer have their career to fall back on. The Purpose Reboot chapter seeks to explore how to rediscover purpose in the next chapter of life by using frameworks like Ikigai and real-life examples of women who have reinvented themselves with clarity and fulfillment.

1. Understanding the Power of Purpose After 55

Why Purpose Matters More Than Ever

Purpose is essential at any age, but after 55, it takes on a new urgency. As people move toward retirement or have more time to focus on their personal lives, they begin to confront the idea of what life is about when they're no longer tied to their career goals or societal expectations. Having a clear sense of purpose can be especially important during this time of life as it helps to provide direction, reduce stress, and boost emotional well-being.

For many, the end of a career can trigger feelings of loss, lack of direction, and anxiety about the future. A study by the University of Michigan found that people who have a strong sense of purpose in life are less likely to experience depression and have a lower risk of death. Purpose acts as a psychological buffer against life's inevitable challenges, providing a sense of meaning in the face of aging, health concerns, and societal change.

Purpose and Aging: The Link to Well-being

The idea of finding meaning after 55 is not just about looking back on a career but about looking forward to the possibilities that lie ahead. While it's true that retirement or transitioning from a lifelong role may bring uncertainty, it also offers the opportunity to reframe how we see ourselves and our place in the world. We can reimagine what it means to live with purpose in this next chapter—whether it's through relationships, hobbies, personal growth, or new ventures. The power of purpose at this stage lies in the ability to reclaim your identity, craft new goals, and contribute to the world in a way that reflects your true values.

Real-life Example:

- Sandra, a 60-year-old teacher, had spent 35 years educating young children. Upon retirement, she faced the challenge of redefining her purpose. Rather than feeling isolated or aimless, Sandra rediscovered her passion for painting, something she had put on hold during her career. Today, Sandra's work is displayed in local galleries, and she hosts art workshops for retirees who are also seeking new forms of self-expression. Through this transition, Sandra found purpose in sharing her art with others, leading her to a fulfilling second career.

2. Ikigai and Other Frameworks for Life Meaning

What is Ikigai?

One powerful framework for finding purpose in life is Ikigai, a Japanese concept that means "a reason for being." It is a holistic approach that integrates four core elements:

1. What you love (your passions)
2. What the world needs (your contributions to society)
3. What you are good at (your talents and strengths)
4. What you can be paid for (your skills and their economic value)

Ikigai encourages individuals to explore the intersection of these four aspects to find balance and meaning in life. It suggests that fulfillment comes not from achieving external markers of success, but from aligning personal passions with the greater good. Ikigai reminds us that even after 55, there's an opportunity to blend skills, interests, and community impact into a satisfying life.

Practical Application of Ikigai

In this phase of life, finding your Ikigai might mean reevaluating the way you've contributed professionally or personally. You may have left behind the career-driven focus and now need to find new ways to fulfill your passions or contribute meaningfully to others.

For example, a retired business executive might realize that their true purpose lies in mentoring young entrepreneurs, while a former nurse might dedicate time to volunteering with health-focused NGOs. Their Ikigai comes not from financial success but from giving back and finding new ways to use their skills for the greater good.

Real-life Example:

- Margaret, a 63-year-old former corporate lawyer, used her retirement to dive into mentorship. Margaret had always enjoyed helping younger colleagues find their way in the profession. Upon retirement, she started offering pro-bono legal advice to underserved communities, focusing on women's rights. Her new purpose came from using her expertise to help others, blending her passion for justice with the needs of the world. Through this work, Margaret discovered the power of aligning what she loved, what she was good at, and what society needed.

Other Frameworks for Meaning

While Ikigai is one well-known framework, several others can help in discovering life meaning after retirement:

- The Fourfold Path of Purpose: This model, developed by Dan Pink, emphasizes the importance of autonomy, mastery, purpose, and connection in crafting a meaningful life. After retirement, you can focus on building autonomy through creative projects or volunteer work, mastering new hobbies or skills, and finding a deep sense of connection with others through community.

- The Great Work: Inspired by Thomas Moore's work, this framework asks individuals to consider their life's "great work", a purpose driven by passion, service, and legacy. This helps retirees see their lives as part of a larger narrative, creating meaningful work that goes beyond day-to-day activities.

3. Real-Life Stories of Women Who Reinvented with Purpose

Turning Adversity into Opportunity

Retirement or career changes often come after years of hard work, and the transition can feel uncertain. Yet, it is through adversity or the void left behind that many women have found their most fulfilling purpose. Here are a few examples of women who reinvented themselves after 55:

- Ruth, a 62-year-old former marketing director, was devastated after being laid off from her job. Rather than succumbing to frustration, Ruth embraced this turning point as an opportunity for reinvention. She began volunteering at a local food bank, helping to organize fundraisers and outreach efforts. Through this work, Ruth found a deep sense of purpose in giving back to her community. She later went on to start her own nonprofit organization dedicated to supporting women in transition after losing their jobs. Ruth's story exemplifies how even in the face of adversity, one can find meaning by helping others and pursuing causes that align with personal values.

- Linda, a 58-year-old retired accountant, had always loved photography but had never pursued it seriously. Upon retiring, she made the decision to finally focus on her passion. She invested in photography equipment, took courses, and began photographing local events. What started as a personal hobby quickly turned into a second career. Today, Linda is a well-respected event photographer who not only enjoys her craft but also mentors younger photographers. Linda's reinvention shows that purpose can be found in pursuing long-lost passions and turning them into a career that offers both joy and purpose.

- Martha, a 64-year-old former teacher, became frustrated by the lack of meaningful retirement activities. She loved working with children and was disappointed when she couldn't find volunteer opportunities that aligned with her skills. So, Martha took the initiative and created an after-school program to teach underprivileged children how to read. Her new venture gave her a renewed sense of purpose and allowed her to continue making a difference in the lives of young people, even after her teaching career had ended.

These women's stories exemplify how retirement is not the end of purpose but a chance to rediscover passion, help others, and build new identities that align with what is meaningful.

Conclusion: Rebooting Purpose in the Second Chapter

The transition into retirement is not about giving up on the future—it's about taking the time to reboot and find deeper meaning in life. By understanding the power of purpose, utilizing frameworks like Ikigai, and learning from the real-life stories of those who have successfully reinvented themselves, we can see that life after 55 offers immense opportunity.

Rather than viewing retirement as a period of loss, it is a time to explore new passions, give back to the community, and find a renewed sense of purpose. Your second act doesn't have to be defined by past roles or expectations—it's a chance to create something that speaks to your true self, brings joy, and makes a difference in the world. The key is to take the first step: embrace the idea that retirement is a reboot, not the end.

DESIGNING YOUR SECOND ACT VISION BOARD

❦

Introduction: A New Beginning—Visualizing Your Second Act

The second act of life—often beginning after retirement—offers a remarkable opportunity for reinvention, fulfillment, and growth. One of the most powerful ways to shape and navigate this transition is through **visualization**. Visualization is more than just an inspirational tool; it's a practical method for organizing your thoughts, aligning your goals, and focusing your energies on the things that matter most to you in this new phase of life.

In this chapter, we will explore the transformative process of creating a **vision board** for your **second act**—a visual map that encapsulates your hopes, dreams, and aspirations. We will also delve into **goal-setting**, ensuring that these goals are designed not just for productivity but for **joy** and **personal fulfillment**. Lastly, we'll guide you through a powerful **vision board or journal exercise** that will help you clarify your intentions and craft a roadmap for a life that's vibrant, meaningful, and purpose-driven.

1. Visualization as a Planning Tool

The Science Behind Visualization

Visualization is a technique rooted in psychology and personal development. It involves mentally picturing a desired outcome or life scenario and then taking steps to make it a reality. Research has shown that visualization can significantly enhance performance, boost confidence, and help in achieving both short-term and long-term goals. The process engages the subconscious mind, which plays a powerful role in shaping our behaviors and decisions.

For many, the idea of creating a vision board feels like a simple activity, but it's far more than just cutting out pictures from magazines and pasting them on a board. It's about clarifying your dreams, aligning your inner values with your outward actions, and creating a life that truly reflects your authentic self.

- The Role of Visualization in Goal Setting: By visualizing your goals, you create a mental blueprint for what you want to achieve. This helps you stay focused on what's important and encourages positive habits that are in alignment with your vision. When you create a vision board, you actively create a connection between the mind, the body, and the outcome you desire.

- Visualization and Neuroplasticity: The brain's ability to reorganize itself in response to new experiences, known as neuroplasticity, can be enhanced by visualization techniques. This means that when you visualize achieving a specific goal or a desired lifestyle, you actually start rewiring your brain to support that goal.

Example:

- Sarah, a 60-year-old retiree, was unsure about her next steps after leaving her long-time career as a teacher. She began using visualization to imagine herself traveling the world and pursuing photography. She created a vision board filled with photos of different countries, cameras, and quotes about exploration and art. This daily practice of visualizing her dream life kept her focused, and within a year, Sarah had started a photography blog, and her travel photos were being sold to magazines.

2. Goal-Setting for Joy, Not Just Productivity

The Importance of Joyful Goals

As you enter your second act, it's crucial to redefine how you set goals. For much of your life, goals may have been driven by external expectations: career advancements, financial stability, or meeting the needs of others. However, retirement and midlife offer a unique opportunity to create goals that are centered on joy, well-being, and personal growth rather than simply productivity and achievement.

When you set goals for joy, you invite a sense of purpose, fulfillment, and satisfaction into your life. The shift from achieving external validation to pursuing internal satisfaction can profoundly affect your mental health, self-esteem, and overall happiness. Setting goals that prioritize self-care, hobbies, relationships, and growth ensures that your second act is not about simply being busy but about living a life that brings true contentment.

Steps to Set Joyful Goals:

- Reflect on What Brings You Joy: The first step in goal-setting for joy is self-reflection. Ask yourself: What makes me feel alive? What activities do I engage in that make time stand still? Whether it's painting, hiking, spending time with loved ones, or learning a new skill, your goals should be centered on what lights you up.

- Shift from Productivity to Purpose: While productivity is important, goals rooted in purpose bring deeper satisfaction. Consider how your goal can align with both your passions and the world around you. For example, if your goal is to travel, how can you make that experience about more than just seeing new places? Could it be about connecting with people, learning a new culture, or photographing landscapes to tell a deeper story?

- Set Small, Manageable Goals: Instead of overwhelming yourself with lofty ambitions, break your goals into smaller, more manageable steps. This helps prevent burnout and makes the process feel more attainable. Small wins lead to larger successes.

Example:

- Tom, 58, wanted to get into gardening after retiring. His initial goal was to start a vegetable garden, but he didn't feel he had the space. After reflecting on his love for gardening and his desire to grow his own food, he set smaller goals—starting with container gardening on his balcony. This small step reignited his passion, and in two years, he was able to grow enough produce to share with neighbors. Tom's experience is a great example of how joy-driven goals lead to fulfillment without the need for grandiose achievements.

3. Vision Board or Journal Exercise

Creating a Vision Board

A vision board is a tangible, visual representation of your goals, dreams, and aspirations. It's an inspiring tool that keeps you focused on what you want to achieve. Creating a vision board for your second act allows you to clarify your intentions and connect with your desires on a deeper level.

Here's how to create your own vision board:

1. Gather Supplies: You'll need a large board (poster board, corkboard, or magnetic board), magazines or printed images, scissors, glue, and markers.

2. Define Your Goals: Reflect on the main themes of your life after retirement—personal growth, hobbies, relationships, travel, health, community, or financial freedom. Consider what makes you feel fulfilled and how you want to contribute to the world.

3. Choose Visuals that Resonate: Cut out pictures, words, or quotes from magazines that represent your goals and dreams. These images should evoke positive emotions and inspiration when you look at them.

4. Arrange Your Vision Board: Start arranging the images on the board. Don't glue anything yet—take your time and play with the layout. Once satisfied, glue everything down.

5. Place the Board Where You Can See It: Display your vision board somewhere visible—on a wall, near your desk, or by your bed. This will serve as a daily reminder of your goals and help you stay motivated.

6. Update Regularly: As you achieve goals, replace old images with new ones to reflect your growth and evolving vision.

Vision Journal Exercise

For those who prefer a more introspective approach, a vision journal is an equally effective tool for goal-setting and visualization. A vision journal allows you to reflect, write, and create a roadmap for your second act.

1. Start with Gratitude: Begin your journal entry by listing things you are grateful for. Acknowledge where you are in life and how far you've come.

2. Describe Your Ideal Second Act: Write a detailed description of what your ideal retirement looks like—be as specific as possible. Describe your daily routine, activities, and relationships. Consider how you want to feel each day.

3. Set Intentions and Goals: Now, set your goals—big or small. Write them down as actionable items and align them with what brings you joy and fulfillment.

4. Visualize Your Success: Spend time visualizing yourself accomplishing these goals. Imagine how you will feel when you achieve them. Write down the emotions that come up.

5. Take Action: End your journal entry by setting the next small step towards making your vision a reality. Start with one small task you can do to move towards your goal.

Real-life Example:

▪ Ellen, a 66-year-old retiree, created a vision board to capture her goals of traveling and learning new languages. After her husband's passing, she felt disconnected and lonely. By setting goals centered on exploration and personal growth, she reignited her passions. Ellen now spends half the year traveling and learning French, and her vision board continues to inspire her daily as she works towards visiting Paris and learning the language fluently.

Conclusion: Designing a Fulfilling Second Act

The second act of life is a time to embrace new opportunities, rediscover old passions, and create a meaningful legacy. Designing a second-act vision board allows you to focus on the positive possibilities that retirement offers. Whether you choose to visualize your goals with a board, a journal, or another tool, the key is to stay intentional about creating a life that aligns with your values, interests, and desires.

Visualization, goal-setting, and the practice of creating vision boards are essential components of this process, providing clarity, motivation, and direction. The second act is your time to shine, and with the tools provided in this chapter, you can start building a life full of purpose, joy, and fulfillment.

By using vision boards and journals, you'll be well on your way to designing a second act that's not just about filling time, but about living with intention and embracing the full potential of this new chapter.

CHAPTER 5

THE POWER OF PASSION PROJECTS AND HOBBIES

~~✦~~

Introduction: Rediscovering Joy and Purpose

In our busy lives, hobbies often take a back seat. We push aside personal interests and creative pursuits to focus on work, family, and obligations. But in retirement or the second act of life, there's an opportunity to breathe new life into those long-lost passions or discover new ones that ignite our spirits. Passion projects and hobbies aren't just distractions—they are the gateway to fulfillment, creativity, and self-expression.

Many people over 55 find that retirement is the perfect time to reconnect with the things they love. Whether it's painting, gardening, woodworking, or cooking, hobbies have the power to bring meaning, balance, and joy into our lives. But they can also be so much more—they can be a source of personal growth, a way to build community, and even turn into successful business ventures.

This chapter explores the power of passion projects and hobbies. It shows how rediscovering long-lost interests can bring us joy, fulfillment, and a sense of purpose. We'll discuss how to start new hobbies that can light you up and provide stories of people who've turned their passions into businesses, demonstrating the untapped potential in activities you love.

1. Turning Long-Lost Interests into Everyday Joy

Why Hobbies Matter

Hobbies are not just for kids or the retired; they are for anyone who seeks a joyful, creative, and fulfilling life. For many of us, life's responsibilities pushed hobbies aside in favor of more "important" tasks. Whether it's due to family commitments, the demands of a career, or simply the hustle and bustle of life, many of us forget about the simple joys that hobbies bring.

- Mental and Physical Benefits: Research consistently shows that hobbies contribute to mental well-being, reduce stress, and even improve cognitive health. For example, activities like reading, painting, or learning a new skill activate different parts of the brain, keeping the mind sharp and engaged.

- Personal Fulfillment: Engaging in a hobby often taps into a deeper sense of personal satisfaction that work or other commitments cannot provide. Hobbies allow us to be in touch with our true selves—our passions, interests, and creativity.

Reconnecting with long-lost hobbies provides an opportunity to rediscover what once made you feel alive. Whether it's something from childhood, like building model airplanes, or something you've always wanted to try, like pottery, the benefits are endless. The time and space that retirement affords can open the door to this personal renaissance.

Tips for Rediscovering Long-Lost Interests

- Reflect on Childhood Passions: Think back to activities you enjoyed as a child. Were you drawn to art, music, nature, or something else? Often, the things that excited us as children can still bring joy and fulfillment as adults. Revisit those old hobbies and see how they might fit into your life now.

- Start Small and Simple: Don't overwhelm yourself with ambitious projects at first. Begin with small steps. If you used to enjoy playing the guitar, dust it off and play for just 15 minutes a day. If you loved painting, set up a small space in your home and begin experimenting with color and form.

- Join Hobbyist Groups: Many communities have local clubs or online groups where people with similar interests come together to share their passion. Joining a group can enhance the enjoyment of your hobby and give you a sense of belonging.

Example:

- Mary, a 62-year-old retiree, had always loved knitting but had set it aside when her children were born. After retiring, she rediscovered her love for knitting and joined an online knitting group. What started as a relaxing hobby turned into an entrepreneurial venture—she now creates and sells handmade scarves and blankets, bringing in extra income while enjoying the creative process.

2. Starting New Hobbies That Light You Up

Why Starting Something New Can Be Life-Changing

While revisiting old passions is rewarding, starting something completely new can have an equally transformative effect. It's a chance to expand your horizons, challenge yourself, and break free from the routine. Taking up new hobbies offers a sense of adventure, providing the opportunity to learn, grow, and rediscover joy.

Starting a new hobby in retirement doesn't require you to completely reinvent yourself—it's about engaging with something that excites you, something that feels new and invigorating. Whether it's learning a new language, trying out photography, or exploring cooking, the possibilities are endless. New hobbies challenge you to grow and create meaning in a way that's not tied to career achievements or external validation.

How to Start a New Hobby

- Identify Interests That Spark Curiosity: Think about areas that interest you but you've never explored. Perhaps you've always wanted to learn about gardening or take up creative writing. The key is to start with curiosity and excitement, not pressure.

- Embrace a Beginner's Mindset: One of the most empowering aspects of starting a new hobby is the freedom it brings. It's okay to be a beginner—don't be afraid of making mistakes or not being perfect. The joy is in the learning process itself.

- Invest in the Right Tools: Some hobbies require specialized equipment or materials. If you're interested in photography, consider investing in a good quality camera. If woodworking is your passion, look into the basic tools you'll need. Remember, hobbies are an investment in yourself.

- Commit to Time for Your Hobby: One of the challenges of starting a new hobby is finding time for it. But retirement gives you the luxury of time. Whether it's dedicating 30 minutes a day or an hour each week, make it a habit and prioritize your hobby.

Example:

- Steve, a 59-year-old retiree, had always admired woodworking but had never tried it himself. After retiring, he enrolled in a local woodworking class and started building small furniture pieces. His hobby soon evolved into a side business—he now sells custom-made furniture to local stores and online. Steve found that his new hobby not only brought him immense satisfaction but also provided him with income and a sense of purpose.

3. Stories of Hobby-to-Business Transformations

Turning a Passion into a Business

One of the most rewarding aspects of pursuing hobbies in retirement is the potential to turn a passion into a business. Many retirees find that their passion projects can not only provide them with personal joy but can also evolve into an income-generating venture. This transformation doesn't have to be immediate— often, it's a gradual process that evolves as you gain skills, build confidence, and find your niche.

The idea of turning a hobby into a business may seem daunting at first, but retirement offers a perfect opportunity to test the waters. The financial pressure isn't the same as it once was, so it becomes a more manageable risk to turn a passion into something more. If done right, your passion can bring in extra income and become a fulfilling part of your life.

How to Turn Your Hobby into a Business

- Find a Market for Your Passion: To transform a hobby into a business, the first step is finding an audience. If you enjoy crafting, consider selling your work at local craft fairs or online platforms like Etsy. If you love baking, perhaps start a small business offering custom cakes for special events.

- Start Small and Scale Gradually: It's important to start small, test the market, and gradually grow your business. Many hobby-to-business stories begin with a side project—just something to see if it resonates with others.

- Invest in Learning: Even though you may already have a lot of expertise in your hobby, running a business requires a different skill set. Consider learning the basics of marketing, pricing, and business management to ensure your passion can thrive as a business.

- Leverage Technology: Use online platforms to reach a broader audience. Setting up a website or using social media can significantly expand your customer base, allowing you to market your work and services beyond local networks.

Real-Life Example:

Janet, a 64-year-old retired marketing manager, always enjoyed making jewelry as a hobby. After retiring, she decided to turn her passion into a business. She began by selling her designs at local craft fairs and quickly found a market for her pieces. Today, Janet has an online jewelry business, selling her creations to customers all over the country. She also mentors other women who want to turn their hobbies into businesses, proving that the right passion can evolve into a thriving career.

Conclusion: Cultivating a Passionate, Purposeful Retirement

The second act of life is the perfect time to cultivate new interests, rediscover lost passions, and explore new avenues of self-expression. Whether you are revisiting old hobbies or starting something entirely new, the possibilities for growth, joy, and personal fulfillment are endless.

By engaging in passion projects and hobbies, you not only find personal satisfaction but also open the door to new opportunities. You may even find that your hobby turns into a business that provides financial rewards and a renewed sense of purpose. The key is to embrace the process, be open to exploration, and allow yourself the freedom to enjoy the journey.

Retirement doesn't signal the end—it's the start of a vibrant new chapter where you can fully immerse yourself in the things that bring you happiness and fulfillment. Your second act can be as dynamic, creative, and rewarding as you choose it to be. Embrace the possibilities that hobbies and passion projects bring, and watch as they transform your retirement into a time of renewal and reinvention.

ENTREPRENEURSHIP AFTER 55—YES, YOU CAN

—◦◦◦◦◦—

Introduction: A New Chapter of Possibilities

R etirement traditionally symbolizes the end of professional responsibilities, a time for rest, leisure, and enjoyment. However, for many, retirement is just the beginning of a new journey, one where the pursuit of purpose and personal fulfillment takes center stage. Far from retreating into a life of passivity, entrepreneurship after 55 offers an exciting opportunity to embrace new challenges, continue growing, and create a business that reflects personal passions and experiences.

In today's world, age is not a barrier to starting a business. In fact, retirees are increasingly taking the leap into entrepreneurship, bringing with them decades of professional experience, wisdom, and an abundance of untapped skills. In this chapter, we will explore why retirement is a fantastic time to launch a business, the practical steps needed to start a side hustle or full-time venture, and hear firsthand stories from women founders who have successfully navigated the entrepreneurial landscape after 55.

1. Why Retirement is a Great Time to Launch a Business

A Fresh Perspective on Work and Purpose

When retirement arrives, many people find themselves with more free time, and the structure that once came with their professional life is no longer there. While this can feel unsettling at first, it also offers the perfect opportunity to reflect, recalibrate, and focus on what really matters—pursuing a passion and building something of your own.

Entrepreneurship after 55 offers the unique chance to embrace autonomy. Many people in their earlier careers were constrained by external factors, including bosses, office politics, and the constant pursuit of promotions. However, in retirement, there's no need for external validation or pressure. You can craft a business that reflects your values, aligns with your passions, and serves a purpose in your life.

Moreover, starting a business in retirement allows you to create something that is deeply personal and meaningful— whether it's a small side hustle that turns into a successful venture or a more ambitious full-time business. In retirement, you don't have to work around the clock, so the pressure of making a business work is balanced with the freedom to explore and pivot until you find the right formula.

Financial Flexibility and Personal Fulfillment

While financial stability is a common motivator for starting a business, many retirees are driven by the desire to create something that is deeply fulfilling. After years of working for a paycheck, it's liberating to pursue an endeavor for its intrinsic rewards, not just the monetary outcome. That's not to say that financial success isn't a goal, but entrepreneurship after 55 allows for a healthier balance between financial aspirations and personal satisfaction.

Additionally, financial security in retirement is a key consideration. Many people approaching retirement have accumulated savings, investments, or a pension, giving them a safety net to start a business without the pressure of immediate income. This financial cushion can make it easier to take calculated risks and grow a business at your own pace.

Skills and Experience That Give You an Edge

Another powerful reason for starting a business after 55 is the wealth of knowledge and skills that retirees bring to the table. After decades of working in a particular field or industry, you have a deep understanding of what works, what doesn't, and what customers or clients truly need. This experience is invaluable, giving you a solid foundation from which to launch your business.

Additionally, the leadership, project management, and organizational skills gained in your career can be directly applied to entrepreneurship. With years of professional experience, you are likely adept at problem-solving, negotiating, and leading teams, all of which are crucial for running a successful business.

2. Practical Steps to Start a "Side Hustle" or Full-Time Venture

Step 1: Identify Your Passion and Niche

The first step in starting a business post-retirement is identifying what you're passionate about. What is it that excites you? What skills do you have that others might need? For some, it's a long-held interest they've put off for years; for others, it's something new that aligns with their evolving lifestyle.

Exercise:

- Make a list of your interests, hobbies, and activities you enjoyed in the past.

- Identify the skills you've gained through your career and life experiences. What can you offer that others might be willing to pay for?

- Consider the market need: Does your idea fulfill a gap or provide a solution to a problem?

Choosing a niche is critical because it helps you narrow your focus and target a specific audience. Whether you decide to focus on handmade jewelry, health coaching, writing, or consulting, make sure there's a market for your product or service.

Step 2: Create a Business Plan

A business plan is essential, even for a small venture or side hustle. It doesn't have to be overly complicated, but it should outline your business model, target audience, pricing strategy, and goals.

The business plan can also serve as a roadmap, guiding you through the initial stages and helping you stay focused on what's important. Key sections of your business plan should include:

- Mission statement: What do you want to accomplish, and why does it matter?

- Market research: Who are your competitors? Who is your target audience?

- Marketing and sales strategy: How will you attract customers or clients?

- Financial projections: How much will you need to start, and what are your revenue goals?

A well-thought-out plan helps mitigate risk and ensures that your business is grounded in a clear strategy.

Step 3: Leverage Technology and Tools

Starting a business today is easier than ever, thanks to the numerous online tools and resources available. Whether you're building a website, managing finances, or marketing your product, there are platforms and software that simplify the process.

For example:

- E-commerce platforms like Shopify, Etsy, or Squarespace provide an easy way to launch an online store.
- Social media platforms like Instagram, Facebook, and Pinterest offer a powerful way to connect with potential customers.
- Financial management tools like QuickBooks or FreshBooks help you track income and expenses.
- Project management tools like Trello or Asana can keep you organized as you grow your business.

While it may feel overwhelming at first, starting small and embracing technology can streamline your business-building process, allowing you to focus on what you do best.

Step 4: Test Your Idea and Build Slowly

Starting a business doesn't have to mean diving in full-time right away. For many retirees, starting a side hustle or part-time venture is a good way to test the waters. This allows you to gauge demand, fine-tune your product or service, and adjust your business strategy before committing fully.

Begin by offering your product or service to a small group of friends, family, or local community members. Use feedback to improve your offerings and fine-tune your approach. You can always scale up once you have validated your business idea and feel confident in its potential.

Step 5: Build a Network and Ask for Help

Entrepreneurship doesn't have to be a solitary endeavor. Building a network of fellow entrepreneurs, mentors, and supporters can provide invaluable guidance, motivation, and resources. Seek out local business organizations, entrepreneurial meetups, or online forums where you can connect with others.

Asking for help is an important part of the process. Whether it's hiring a consultant to assist with marketing or reaching out to friends who have business experience, don't be afraid to tap into your network for support.

3. Interview Snippets from Women Founders Post-Retirement

Case Study 1: Susan, Founder of GreenTech Solutions

Susan, 62, was a former environmental consultant who retired after 40 years in the industry. But she soon realized that retirement wasn't the right fit for her. Instead of slowing down, she decided to start a business focused on sustainable living solutions—something she had always been passionate about.

"I felt like I still had so much to give," says Susan. "Retirement doesn't mean you stop growing. In fact, it's a chance to dive deeper into what you truly care about. My business isn't just about making money; it's about leaving a legacy of sustainability for future generations."

Susan started by offering consulting services to businesses looking to improve their environmental impact. Over the years, her company expanded to include eco-friendly products and green energy solutions. She credits the support of her network and her deep knowledge of the industry for her business's success.

Case Study 2: Linda, Creator of Handmade Jewelry Line

At 58, Linda decided to leave her career as a corporate trainer and follow her passion for jewelry-making. "I had always loved working with my hands, but I never had the time while I was working full-time," Linda shares. "Retirement gave me the freedom to finally focus on something I loved."

Linda started small, selling her pieces at local markets and on social media. Her handmade jewelry business has since grown, and she now ships internationally. "It's not just about selling jewelry—it's about creating something that makes people feel beautiful," she says. Linda's story is a perfect example of how passion can translate into a thriving business, regardless of age.

Conclusion: Embrace Entrepreneurship After 55

The entrepreneurial journey after 55 may seem daunting, but it is an incredibly rewarding and empowering experience. With the right mindset, practical steps, and a willingness to learn, it is possible to build a business that brings both financial success and personal fulfillment.

Whether you're starting a small side hustle or building a full-time venture, remember that retirement is an opportunity for reinvention. The skills, wisdom, and experiences you've gained over the years can now be channeled into something new, exciting, and meaningful.

Take inspiration from the stories shared in this chapter, and embrace the possibilities. Entrepreneurship after 55 isn't just a way to stay busy—it's a chance to live with purpose and passion, proving that age is no barrier to creating something extraordinary. Yes, you can—and this is just the beginning.

CHAPTER 7

LIFELONG LEARNING—BRAINS DON'T EXPIRE

❦

Introduction: The Journey of Continuous Growth

The concept of lifelong learning is not a new one, but it is becoming increasingly vital as society evolves. Traditionally, learning has been associated with school, university, or professional development. But what happens when we retire or reach later stages of life? Does the opportunity for learning stop? Absolutely not. In fact, this is the time when the joy of becoming a student again can be the most fulfilling and rewarding.

As we age, many of us start to experience a change in our cognitive landscape. While it's true that our physical bodies age, the human brain remains incredibly plastic, meaning it can still change and adapt throughout our lives. This chapter explores the power of lifelong learning, how to embrace becoming a student again after 55, and the endless opportunities for growth that exist for those ready to keep learning.

Learning not only keeps our minds sharp but also enriches our lives, making us more engaged and fulfilled. It opens doors to new experiences, skills, and passions. For many retirees, lifelong learning represents a golden opportunity to engage with the world in fresh, exciting ways. Whether it's through formal courses, self-study, or "edu-vacations," the possibilities are endless.

1. Embracing the Joy of Becoming a Student Again

Why Learning Never Stops

As we age, it's easy to believe that we have learned enough—that there's no need to continue studying, exploring, or expanding our minds. However, research shows that lifelong learning has numerous benefits, including improving cognitive function, delaying the onset of mental decline, and increasing life satisfaction. The joy of learning isn't limited to the classroom. It can be found in self-driven exploration, creative pursuits, and even hands-on experiences.

- Mental Agility and Neuroplasticity: Contrary to popular belief, the brain doesn't lose its ability to change as we age. In fact, studies show that lifelong learning stimulates neuroplasticity, the process through which the brain forms new neural connections. Whether it's learning a new language, mastering a musical instrument, or solving puzzles, each new challenge helps to strengthen the brain.

- Personal Fulfillment: Learning allows us to explore interests that we may have neglected or forgotten in the hustle of our careers. Whether it's finally taking up that long-desired hobby or tackling a complex topic, the personal satisfaction that comes from learning is unparalleled.

- Building New Skills: In a world that's constantly evolving, staying current is essential. Lifelong learning provides the opportunity to acquire new skills—be it through tech workshops, online courses, or experiential learning—and to remain relevant and competent in an increasingly digital world.

The Shift in Mindset

Adopting the mindset of a lifetime learner requires a shift away from the idea that education is a formal process reserved for the young. Instead, it's about recognizing that curiosity and growth don't have an expiration date. Lifelong learning means embracing exploration and self-discovery—traits that are timeless and can lead to unexpected joys.

- Overcoming Fear of Technology: Many older adults feel intimidated by modern technology, but this is an excellent opportunity to embrace new tools. Learning how to navigate smartphones, apps, and social media can open doors to online education, global communities, and a host of learning platforms.

- Exploring New Territories: Just because you're retiring doesn't mean you have to slow down mentally. Pursue what excites you—whether it's photography, writing, learning a new language, or exploring global cultures. Embrace being a student again, without the pressure or constraints of formal schooling.

Real-Life Example:

- John, a retired lawyer in his late 60s, took up painting after retirement, something he'd always been curious about but never had time for. Initially intimidated by the idea of being a beginner, John found a local art class and began learning. Over time, he became quite skilled and even started showcasing his work at local galleries. John's story is a testament to how embracing learning after 55 can lead to unexpected joy, personal growth, and even a new passion that becomes a part of your identity.

2. Free and Affordable Learning Resources for Older Adults

Accessing Knowledge Without the Price Tag

The idea that education costs must be prohibitive is increasingly outdated. Today, a wealth of free and affordable resources is available to older adults looking to continue their learning journey. These resources not only make learning accessible but also flexible, so you can learn at your own pace, on your terms.

- Online Learning Platforms: Many universities and organizations offer free courses online. Websites like Coursera, edX, and FutureLearn provide a wide range of courses from top universities. Subjects include everything from history to data science, languages, and even personal development.

- Public Libraries: Public libraries are incredible resources for lifelong learners. Many libraries offer free online courses, access to eBooks, audiobooks, and educational programs. Libraries also often provide free access to platforms like Lynda.com (now LinkedIn Learning), which offers a wide array of technical courses.

- YouTube: A free and underutilized resource, YouTube has endless tutorials and educational content on virtually any subject. Whether you're learning to cook, sew, or understand the stock market, YouTube provides free access to expert-led content.

- MOOCs (Massive Open Online Courses): MOOCs are open-access educational platforms that offer free courses on everything from personal finance to art history. Examples of popular MOOC platforms include Khan Academy,

Udemy, and MIT OpenCourseWare. These platforms offer an easy way for older adults to explore new subjects without any financial commitment.

- Social Media Groups and Forums: Online communities and forums can also be great places to learn. Websites like Reddit, Facebook Groups, and Quora provide opportunities for individuals to ask questions, share knowledge, and engage in educational discussions. Many groups specifically cater to older adults or people looking to learn new skills.

Real-Life Example:

- Carol, a 67-year-old retiree, had always wanted to learn more about technology but felt overwhelmed by the subject. She discovered Coursera, which offered free courses on basic computing and digital literacy. After completing a few courses, she felt confident navigating her devices, which helped her stay connected with friends and family through video calls and social media. Carol's story shows that access to free resources can empower individuals to acquire valuable skills in their later years.

3. Travel + Education = "Edu-Vacations"

The Rise of Edu-Vacations

As the world becomes increasingly interconnected, the idea of combining education and travel is gaining popularity. More and more people are embarking on edu-vacations, a hybrid of travel and learning where the journey itself becomes an educational experience. Edu-vacations allow retirees to explore new cultures, languages, or topics of personal interest, all while enriching their lives and creating unforgettable experiences.

These trips are designed to promote learning while experiencing the world's diversity. Whether you're taking a cooking class in Italy, a history tour in Greece, or learning yoga in India, edu-vacations allow you to immerse yourself in different cultures while gaining new knowledge and skills.

Types of Edu-Vacations

- Cultural Immersion Trips: Travel to countries where you can engage deeply with the culture. This could mean participating in language courses in Spain, art classes in France, or cooking workshops in Thailand. These trips allow you to learn while living within the local community.

- Historical and Educational Tours: Visit historical landmarks and museums while receiving lectures or guided tours from experts. For example, you could visit the Ancient Ruins of Rome or explore African history in Egypt, learning from passionate historians and academics.

- Creative Retreats: Many retreats offer an immersive environment where you can focus on a creative hobby, such as writing, painting, or photography, all while being surrounded by nature or a beautiful historical setting. These retreats foster both personal development and creativity.

- Skill-building Experiences: You could travel to locations where you can learn specific skills like pottery-making, farming, bird-watching, or even meditation. These experiences allow you to broaden your skills while enjoying new environments.

Benefits of Edu-Vacations

- Engaging with New Cultures: Edu-vacations immerse you in new cultures, giving you the opportunity to learn first-hand about different ways of life.

- Building Confidence: Traveling and learning in a different setting pushes you out of your comfort zone, helping you build confidence and adaptability.

- Reconnecting with Yourself: Learning something new in a new environment often helps individuals reconnect with themselves and rediscover passions they may have set aside in earlier years.

- Social Connection: Edu-vacations offer opportunities to meet like-minded people, expanding your network and building new friendships with those who share similar interests.

Real-life Example:

- Barbara, a 60-year-old retiree, combined her love of travel and learning by taking a month-long trip to France. She enrolled in a language immersion program and spent her days learning French, while exploring the picturesque towns of Provence. The trip not only improved her language skills but also enriched her life in ways she never imagined. Today, Barbara continues to travel and enroll in educational programs that fulfill her curiosity and bring her joy.

Conclusion: The Power of Lifelong Learning

Lifelong learning is one of the greatest gifts you can give yourself, especially in the later years of life. Whether it's by revisiting old passions, learning new skills, or exploring the world through edu-vacations, the possibilities are limitless.

Your brain doesn't expire—it continues to evolve, grow, and adapt. By embracing the joy of becoming a student again, you open yourself up to a world of endless possibilities and untapped potential. Learning becomes an ongoing journey that nurtures curiosity, creativity, and well-being. It keeps you engaged in life and provides purpose, fulfillment, and new challenges to look forward to.

So, let this chapter be a reminder that the second act of life doesn't mean slowing down. Instead, it's a time to keep learning, keep growing, and keep thriving. No matter your age, the world is full of knowledge, and it's waiting for you to explore. Keep learning, and your second act will be one of boundless discovery and excitement.

MIND & MOOD—EMOTIONAL WELLNESS IN THE GOLDEN YEARS

⊸⋙❦⋘⊷

Introduction: The Emotional Landscape of Aging

The process of aging brings with it a unique blend of experiences, both rewarding and challenging. For many, retirement marks a new chapter of freedom, self-discovery, and fulfillment. However, it can also bring about emotional challenges like anxiety, loneliness, and the stress of significant life transitions. While many older adults experience these feelings as a natural part of aging, they don't have to define your quality of life. Just as physical wellness requires attention and care, so too does emotional wellness.

This chapter will explore the intricacies of emotional well-being as we age. We will focus on common emotional hurdles like anxiety, loneliness, and the emotional impact of major life transitions. From there, we'll dive into mental wellness rituals you can integrate into your daily life to support and nurture your emotional health. Lastly, we will discuss when to seek help, how to find support, and why taking care of your mental health is not just important but essential for living a fulfilling, joyful life in your golden years.

1. Managing Anxiety, Loneliness, and Big Transitions

Anxiety in Later Life: What It Looks Like

Anxiety is a common emotional challenge among older adults. While it can be triggered by specific situations—such as retirement or health concerns—sometimes anxiety manifests without a clear cause, simply as a feeling of unease about the unknown. In this stage of life, individuals may worry about things like financial security, family dynamics, and losing independence. Anxiety can present itself in many ways, such as restlessness, trouble sleeping, difficulty concentrating, or physical symptoms like increased heart rate or muscle tension.

It's important to acknowledge that while some level of anxiety is natural during big life transitions, it can become overwhelming and interfere with daily life if not managed properly. The good news is that there are many ways to alleviate anxiety and improve emotional resilience.

Loneliness: The Hidden Epidemic

Loneliness is another emotional challenge that often accompanies aging. As we age, we may experience changes in our social circles, such as the loss of close friends, partners, or even family members. Retirement may also result in a loss of daily social interactions that work once provided. For many, the absence of a clear social structure can lead to feelings of isolation and loneliness.

Loneliness isn't just about being physically alone—it's also about feeling disconnected from others. It's important to recognize that feeling lonely doesn't mean you're unlovable or that you can't form meaningful relationships. Instead, loneliness is often about finding the right connections and ensuring that your emotional needs are met.

Big Transitions: Retirement, Relocation, and Health Changes

The transition into retirement is a major life shift, and while it can be incredibly fulfilling, it can also create feelings of uncertainty or loss. For many, retirement signifies the end of a long-standing professional identity, which can feel like losing a sense of purpose. Retirement can also bring other changes, such as relocation to a new city, downsizing, or coping with health issues or physical limitations. These transitions require emotional adjustment and resilience, and often, support in navigating them.

It's not uncommon for older adults to struggle with finding meaning or purpose post-retirement. Moreover, physical changes in health can also affect emotional health, leading to frustration or sadness about the loss of mobility or vitality. Understanding that these emotional challenges are part of the natural aging process can be helpful. There's nothing wrong with feeling overwhelmed, and it's crucial to take steps to manage these emotions in a healthy way.

Real-Life Example:

- Barbara, a 62-year-old retiree, struggled with loneliness after her husband passed away and her adult children moved out of town. She found it difficult to adjust to her new reality, and the loss of her social network triggered anxiety. Over time, Barbara decided to join a local book club and volunteer at a community center. These social activities helped her develop a sense of belonging and connection, alleviating much of her loneliness and helping her build a new social circle.

2. Daily Mental Wellness Rituals

The Power of Rituals for Emotional Health

One of the most effective ways to manage emotional well-being is by implementing daily mental wellness rituals. These practices help ground you, reduce anxiety, and cultivate a sense of balance and peace. By committing to rituals that support your emotional health, you create a sense of routine, stability, and control, which are especially important during times of transition or stress.

Some of these daily rituals are simple, yet profoundly effective:

- Mindfulness Meditation: Practicing mindfulness meditation for even 10-15 minutes a day can help reduce stress and anxiety. Mindfulness teaches you to focus on the present moment, allowing you to observe your thoughts and emotions without judgment. Studies have shown that regular meditation can help decrease symptoms of depression and anxiety, improve sleep quality, and reduce overall stress levels.

- Journaling: Journaling is a powerful tool for self-reflection and emotional processing. Writing down your thoughts can help you understand your feelings, reflect on your day, and identify patterns of stress or worry. Journaling also encourages gratitude, which has been shown to improve mental health by shifting focus away from stressors and towards what's positive in life.

- Physical Exercise: Exercise is not only beneficial for physical health but is also crucial for emotional wellness. Regular physical activity boosts the production of endorphins, which are known as the body's "feel-good" hormones. Exercise has been linked to lower levels of anxiety and depression and improved mood. Whether it's going for a walk, doing yoga, or attending a fitness class, physical movement is an essential part of mental health.

- Deep Breathing Exercises: Deep breathing exercises are a simple yet effective way to activate the parasympathetic nervous system, which is responsible for the body's relaxation response. By practicing deep breathing techniques, such as diaphragmatic breathing or 4-7-8 breathing, you can reduce anxiety, lower your heart rate, and calm your mind.

- Creative Activities: Engaging in creative pursuits like painting, writing, or crafting can help reduce stress and provide an outlet for expression. Creative activities allow you to focus your energy on something productive and joyful, promoting emotional health through relaxation and engagement.

Real-Life Example:

- Edward, 66, started practicing mindfulness meditation after feeling increasingly overwhelmed by anxiety and uncertainty following his retirement. He set aside 15 minutes each morning to meditate, focusing on his breath and being present in the moment. Over time, Edward noticed a significant decrease in his anxiety levels and found that he could approach challenges with greater calm and clarity.

3. When to Seek Help and How to Find Support

Recognizing When You Need Help

Despite the many tools available for managing emotional wellness, there are times when the support of mental health professionals is necessary. Seeking help is not a sign of weakness—it's an important step towards taking care of yourself. Whether you're struggling with anxiety, depression, or simply need someone to talk to, professional support can provide the guidance and tools to navigate these challenges.

Some signs that it might be time to seek help include:

- Persistent feelings of hopelessness or helplessness
- Difficulty managing day-to-day tasks due to emotional distress
- Persistent anxiety or panic attacks
- A lack of interest in previously enjoyable activities, including socializing or hobbies
- Difficulty maintaining relationships due to emotional strain
- Physical symptoms like fatigue, sleep disturbances, or changes in appetite linked to emotional distress

It's important to seek professional help if you're experiencing any of the above symptoms, as untreated mental health issues can impact both emotional well-being and physical health.

How to Find Support

The good news is that support is available in many forms, and finding the right resources is a key part of healing and emotional wellness.

- Therapy and Counseling: Therapy can be a life-changing tool for addressing emotional struggles. Cognitive Behavioral Therapy (CBT), for example, is widely used to help individuals manage anxiety, depression, and other emotional challenges. A trained therapist can help you identify negative thought patterns and provide strategies for coping with them.

- Support Groups: Many people find comfort in joining support groups where they can connect with others going through similar experiences. Whether online or in-person, these groups offer a sense of community and understanding that can alleviate feelings of isolation and loneliness.

- Helplines and Crisis Services: National helplines and local crisis services are available to offer immediate support during times of acute emotional distress. These services provide confidential support and can connect you to mental health resources.

- Physical Health Care Providers: If emotional struggles are impacting your physical health, it's important to reach out to your primary care physician. Many healthcare providers are trained to recognize symptoms of emotional distress and can provide referrals to therapists or counselors.

Real-Life Example:

- Louise, 68, struggled with feelings of depression and isolation after losing her spouse. She had always prided herself on being independent, but eventually, her emotional state began to affect her ability to function. After months of trying to manage on her own, she reached out to a counselor and began attending a grief support group. Louise found that talking about her feelings and learning new coping mechanisms helped her heal emotionally. She now actively participates in the group and encourages others to seek support when they need it.

Conclusion: Embracing Emotional Wellness in the Golden Years

Emotional wellness is a lifelong pursuit, but it's especially important in our later years. By managing anxiety, loneliness, and life's transitions with mindfulness, daily rituals, and seeking professional support when needed, we can embrace emotional health in a holistic and empowering way.

The golden years are meant to be a time of peace, fulfillment, and continued growth. By taking steps to care for our mental health, we ensure that we can fully enjoy the opportunities that come with aging—new hobbies, stronger relationships, and an ongoing sense of purpose. Remember, emotional wellness is not a destination but a journey—one that is supported by daily practices, meaningful connections, and the willingness to reach out when needed.

CHAPTER 9

FRIENDSHIPS, SISTERHOOD & BUILDING NEW CIRCLES

———— ❧ ————

Introduction: The Importance of Connection in Later Life

As we enter our 50s and 60s, the dynamic of our friendships can change drastically. We may experience losses, or feel the growing distance between us and old friends due to life circumstances like relocation, family obligations, or personal transformations. However, with these changes comes a powerful opportunity to build new relationships and strengthen existing ones.

For women, friendships aren't just about companionship—they are essential to emotional health, happiness, and longevity. As we age, social connections become more important than ever. Whether it's reconnecting with old friends, building a sisterhood, or forming new social circles, making and nurturing friendships in later life brings joy and purpose. In this chapter, we'll explore how to make new friends after 55, the transformative power of female friendships at this stage, and practical tips for hosting, networking, and staying socially engaged.

1. How to Make New Friends After 55

Understanding the Challenges

Making new friends after 55 can feel like an overwhelming task. As we age, it can become harder to meet people due to various factors, such as:

- Changing Social Circles: Many people lose touch with old friends due to life transitions such as retirement, children leaving home, or even the death of close friends or spouses.

- Limited Opportunities: Post-retirement, people often have fewer daily interactions that lead to organic friendship-building. Workplaces, social clubs, and other structured environments that once fostered friendships may no longer exist.

- Increased Self-Awareness: As we mature, we often have a more refined sense of who we are and what we value, which can make finding compatible friends feel like a challenge.

However, despite these obstacles, the desire for connection remains strong, and there are many ways to cultivate new friendships in later life.

Steps to Building New Friendships

1. Put Yourself Out There The first step to making new friends is putting yourself in situations where you can meet people. This could mean joining local clubs, attending community events, or engaging in online groups centered around your interests. It might feel uncomfortable at first, but being proactive and consistent is key.

   - Volunteer: Volunteering not only provides an opportunity to give back but also allows you to meet like-minded individuals who share your values.

- ○ Enroll in Classes: Whether it's a language class, fitness class, or book club, educational or recreational classes offer natural opportunities to bond with others over a shared interest.

2. Embrace Vulnerability Building meaningful friendships requires a certain level of vulnerability. Being open about your feelings, your past, and your current needs can create authentic connections. Don't be afraid to share your experiences and listen to others do the same. True friendship is rooted in mutual trust and understanding.

3. Find Common Ground When meeting new people, focus on finding common ground. Shared experiences, values, or goals can form the basis of a strong friendship. Ask open-ended questions, listen actively, and be genuinely curious about others' lives.

4. Leverage Technology Social media platforms and online communities have made it easier to find and connect with people from all over the world. Sites like Facebook, Meetup, and Bumble BFF can be excellent tools for making new friends in your area. Many women over 55 find that online spaces provide them with the flexibility to connect without the pressure of traditional social settings.

Real-Life Example:

- Martha, a 58-year-old retiree, found that her close-knit circle of friends had started to diminish as they moved to different cities or passed away. Instead of feeling isolated, Martha decided to join a local hiking group. Over time, she built meaningful relationships with fellow hikers who shared her love of nature. These new friendships have enriched her life, giving her regular opportunities for connection and adventure.

2. The Power of Female Friendship in This Phase of Life

Why Female Friendships Are Especially Important After 55

Female friendships are not only a source of companionship but also emotional support, self-discovery, and personal growth. Research shows that women often place a higher value on social connections than men and benefit more from these relationships, especially in later life. Friendships between women help combat feelings of loneliness, depression, and anxiety.

- Emotional Support: Friendships offer a safe space for sharing personal challenges, joys, and fears. They provide the emotional validation needed to navigate difficult life transitions like loss, health changes, or retirement.

- Social Engagement: Engaging in social activities with friends helps reduce isolation and can improve both mental and physical health. Studies show that women who maintain strong social connections tend to have lower levels of stress and a lower risk of chronic illness.

- Shared Wisdom and Experience: As women age, they often find that their friendships offer a sense of belonging and understanding that is rooted in shared experiences. These relationships allow them to learn from each other, grow emotionally, and support each other's aspirations.

Creating a Sisterhood

Creating a sisterhood is about building deep, trusting relationships with other women who support one another unconditionally. This connection goes beyond casual friendships and forms a community of women who offer emotional and practical support through life's challenges.

- Cultivate Deep Conversations: Going beyond surface-level interactions and engaging in meaningful discussions fosters intimacy and trust.
- Celebrate Each Other's Achievements: A healthy sisterhood supports individual goals and achievements. Celebrating one another's successes, no matter how small, strengthens the bond between friends.

The Positive Impact of Friendships on Mental Health

Friendships also have a positive impact on mental health. Women in their 50s and 60s who maintain close friendships report lower stress levels, better mental clarity, and higher levels of self-esteem. These relationships also serve as important sounding boards during times of self-reflection and can guide you in making major life decisions.

Real-Life Example:

- Helen, 63, experienced a difficult divorce and struggled with loneliness and low self-esteem. After finding a support group for women going through similar experiences, she formed close friendships that helped her rebuild her confidence and sense of self-worth. The friendships became a lifeline as she navigated life as a single woman in her 60s.

3. Tips for Hosting, Networking, and Staying Social

Hosting Events to Strengthen Friendships

Hosting gatherings is a fantastic way to deepen your connections and stay socially engaged. It doesn't have to be anything extravagant—a simple dinner or coffee meetup can foster deeper connections. Hosting also creates an opportunity for friends to meet each other, expanding your network of supportive individuals.

- Organize Small Gatherings: Host a small dinner, tea party, or game night at your home. These intimate gatherings allow for more personal connections and meaningful conversations.
- Celebrate Milestones: Use birthdays, anniversaries, or retirement parties as an excuse to bring people together. Celebrating milestones strengthens bonds and gives everyone something to look forward to.

Networking: Finding New Circles of Influence

Networking isn't just for the younger generation. In fact, social networking after 55 can be incredibly beneficial for meeting new people and cultivating new friendships. Many women find that joining community organizations, clubs, or volunteer groups opens the door to a world of new social opportunities.

- Professional Networking: Even in retirement, many women continue to network for personal and professional growth. Attending industry events, conferences, or meet-ups related to a past career or a new venture provides an opportunity to expand your social circle.
- Civic and Volunteer Work: Many older adults find fulfillment in volunteering, which naturally leads to meeting like-minded individuals who share similar values and interests.

Staying Social with Technology

Technology plays a pivotal role in staying socially connected in today's world. Learning to use video calls, social media, and messaging apps helps bridge the gap when face-to-face meetings aren't possible. Setting up virtual hangouts or joining online groups based on shared interests allows you to stay connected no matter where you are.

Real-Life Example:

- Lillian, 60, had always been active in her book club but found it difficult to meet in person after moving to a new city. She turned to Zoom to keep the book club alive, organizing virtual meetings with friends from her old town. The virtual meetings became a lifeline during the pandemic and provided a consistent source of connection and joy.

Conclusion: Embracing New Connections and Expanding Your Circle

As we age, the need for connection doesn't diminish—it becomes even more critical to our overall health and well-being. The friendships you cultivate in your golden years can bring immense joy, a sense of belonging, and emotional support that enriches your life.

Building new friendships after 55 is not only possible but incredibly rewarding. By putting yourself out there, being vulnerable, and joining communities that align with your passions, you can create lasting, meaningful relationships that continue to grow and evolve. Remember, friendship isn't just about spending time together—it's about supporting each other, sharing experiences, and growing together.

Your sisterhood can be a source of strength, comfort, and joy—it's never too late to build a circle of women who will be there for you, just as you will be there for them. So embrace the power of friendship, stay socially engaged, and allow the connections you build to enrich your life in ways you never imagined.

LOVE, SEX, AND DATING AFTER RETIREMENT

Introduction: Embracing New Beginnings in Love and Intimacy

Retirement doesn't just signify the end of one's professional journey—it also opens the door to a new chapter in personal life, where love, sex, and intimacy can take on new meaning. As we age, many aspects of our lives change, including how we view romance and intimacy. For some, it's a time to rediscover passion, rekindle relationships, or even explore new romantic possibilities. For others, it may be an opportunity to embrace the freedom and joy of being single and starting anew.

As we navigate these later years, it's important to understand that love and intimacy don't diminish with age—in fact, they can evolve into something more fulfilling, profound, and deeply satisfying. This chapter will explore how to redefine romance and intimacy in retirement, share dating tips for those who have experienced loss or are new to the dating scene, and offer advice for couples on how to keep the spark alive in long-term relationships. Whether you're embracing the idea of dating again or nurturing a long-term commitment, the possibilities for love and connection are limitless.

1. Redefining Romance and Intimacy in Later Life

The Evolving Nature of Romance

Romance and intimacy are often seen as things for the young, but that perception is changing. In fact, the golden years are one of the best times to redefine what romance means. As you get older, the pressures of raising children, building a career, and navigating the stresses of life fade. This opens up the possibility to connect more deeply with yourself and your partner, cultivating intimacy in a way that feels authentic and enriching.

The idea of romance in later life isn't about grand gestures or "flower petal" moments, though these can still have their place. It's about gentle connection, spending quality time together, and discovering new ways to bond. Many people find that as they mature, they have a greater appreciation for intimacy—both emotional and physical—that transcends youthful attraction and moves toward deeper connection and mutual respect.

- Emotional Intimacy: As we age, we often have the freedom to move beyond the superficial aspects of relationships and dive into deeper, more meaningful conversations. Intimacy in later life is about vulnerability, honesty, and truly understanding one another. It's about sharing life's journey together, understanding each other's fears, dreams, and experiences, and providing unwavering support.

- Physical Intimacy: As we age, there can be physical changes that affect sexual intimacy, such as hormone shifts, changes in sexual drive, or health issues. However, these changes don't mean the end of physical connection. Many older couples find that as they mature, their sexual experiences become more relaxed and intimate, focusing on connection rather than performance. Exploring non-sexual forms of affection, such as holding hands, cuddling, or just sitting together in silence, can also foster closeness.

Building a Relationship That Nourishes Your Soul

In later life, intimacy can be about nurturing each other's emotional and psychological well-being. It's about being there for each other, providing emotional support during difficult times, and celebrating each other's achievements and joys. The foundation of intimacy at this stage of life is often based on mutual respect, deep understanding, and shared values.

In fact, many people find that they are able to communicate more openly with their partners after retirement. Without the daily pressures of work and raising children, there's more time for meaningful conversation, self-reflection, and alignment of future goals.

Real-Life Example:

- Jack and Barbara, both in their 60s, had been married for over 30 years, but once they both retired, they found that their relationship had taken on a new dynamic. With the kids grown and moved out, they realized they had spent decades focused on others and not enough time on each other. So, they started taking weekend trips together, joined a wine-tasting club, and even took cooking classes. These activities helped them discover new dimensions of their relationship, and they found that their bond had deepened in ways they hadn't expected.

2. Dating Tips for Widowed, Divorced, or Curious Single Women

Embracing the Possibility of New Love

For many women over 55, the idea of entering the dating world after a divorce, the death of a partner, or simply after years of being focused on family and career can feel daunting. But it's also an exciting opportunity to reclaim your personal freedom and explore the possibility of finding love again.

Dating after 55 doesn't mean you're chasing youth or trying to recreate a past love. It means embracing the present, celebrating the person you've become, and finding a partner who appreciates you for who you are now.

- Start Slow and Be Open: If you're re-entering the dating scene after a significant loss or break-up, it's important to take things slowly. There's no rush to jump into a relationship, and being open to dating casually at first can give you the space to learn what you truly want in a partner. Online dating apps or matchmaking services geared toward older adults are great places to start. Sites like Match.com, OurTime, and eHarmony have specific platforms for people over 50, allowing you to meet others who are in a similar life stage.

- Be Authentic: After decades of relationships, you have a clear sense of who you are. Use this knowledge to be authentic in your approach to dating. Let go of the pressure to be someone you're not, and instead, embrace who you are now—flaws, quirks, and all. Being authentic will attract people who appreciate you for the person you've become.

- Embrace New Experiences: Dating in later life may feel different, but that doesn't mean it can't be fun and fulfilling. Try new activities with potential partners. Go for walks, try cooking together, or attend events that interest you. Dating after 55 is an opportunity to experience new aspects of romance and partnership, even if you're not seeking to settle down.

- Set Healthy Boundaries: As we age, we often become more comfortable with setting healthy boundaries in relationships. This is especially true in the dating world. If something doesn't feel right, or you're unsure about a potential partner, don't be afraid to walk away. Your emotional health is paramount, and dating should never feel like a source of stress or discomfort.

Real-Life Example:

- Linda, 60, had been widowed for 5 years and wasn't sure if she was ready to date again. However, after joining a local book club and meeting someone who shared her interests, she began to feel more open to the idea. They started with casual meetings for coffee and gradually moved toward longer outings. Over time, Linda found that dating again had given her the confidence to rediscover love on her terms.

3. Keeping the Spark Alive in Long-Term Partnerships

Maintaining Connection Over Time

In long-term relationships, whether through marriage or long-term partnerships, maintaining intimacy and keeping the spark alive can become challenging as time goes on. Over the years, daily routines, family commitments, and even physical changes can create emotional distance between partners.

However, with intention and effort, it's possible to reignite passion and maintain emotional and physical intimacy, no matter how many years have passed.

- Nurture Emotional Intimacy: Emotional intimacy is the cornerstone of a strong relationship. It requires open communication, understanding, and empathy. Check in with each other regularly, not just about the day-to-day details, but about your dreams, fears, and needs. Share how you feel about the relationship and actively listen to your partner's feelings as well.

- Make Time for Each Other: As life progresses, it's easy to fall into the trap of taking your partner for granted. Prioritize spending quality time together. Whether it's going on date nights, taking vacations, or simply spending time in the kitchen preparing a meal together, intentional moments can help maintain the connection.

- Keep the Physical Connection Alive: Physical intimacy is often one of the first aspects of a relationship to fade, but it's a critical component of a healthy relationship. This doesn't mean focusing solely on sex; simple acts of affection like holding hands, hugging, or cuddling can help keep the physical connection strong. If physical intimacy has been a challenge due to age or health issues, discuss ways to adapt and explore new forms of affection together.

- Try New Things Together: After many years together, partners may fall into a routine. To reignite the spark, try something new—take a dance class, go on an adventure trip, or start a new hobby together. Shared experiences help partners bond and create new memories.

Real-Life Example:

- Eva and Bill, both in their 70s, had been married for over 45 years. After retiring, they found themselves feeling emotionally distant. To reconnect, they decided to take painting classes together. The shared experience helped them rediscover their love for each other, and their renewed intimacy became an important part of their relationship. Their story is an example of how new experiences and shared activities can help rekindle love and intimacy.

Conclusion: Embracing Love, Sex, and Dating in the Golden Years

Retirement is a time to embrace the possibilities that love, intimacy, and connection bring. Whether you're rediscovering a long-term partner or starting a new chapter in your dating life, the golden years offer unique opportunities to redefine and explore romance and intimacy. The key is to stay open to the possibilities—to create authentic connections, nurture your relationships, and remain committed to keeping the spark alive.

In later life, love isn't just about the thrill of new romance or the excitement of physical intimacy. It's about deep emotional bonds, mutual respect, and the ability to share your authentic self with someone who sees and values you for who you are now.

So, whether you're enjoying a thriving relationship or seeking out new connections, remember: love and intimacy are lifelong journeys, not destinations. And in your golden years, those journeys are filled with boundless opportunities for connection, growth, and joy.

CHAPTER 11

HEALTH IS WEALTH—MOVING, EATING, AND THRIVING

❧

Introduction: The Link Between Health and Longevity

As we age, health takes on a new level of importance. For many, the focus shifts from staying young to living well. At 55 and beyond, the way we care for our bodies becomes the cornerstone of maintaining a high quality of life. We are no longer just looking to extend life, but to enrich it. Health is wealth, and it is up to us to create sustainable habits that promote physical, mental, and emotional well-being.

The truth is, many people in their 50s, 60s, and beyond have the opportunity to enjoy their best years yet. By embracing movement, nutritious food, and self-care routines, we can enhance our vitality, preserve our mobility, and thrive in our golden years.

In this chapter, we will explore how to create a realistic wellness routine that focuses on movement, fitness, and nutrition. We will emphasize how these elements work together to provide lasting vitality and optimize health as we age.

1. Creating a Realistic Wellness Routine

Understanding the Need for a Routine After 55

At 55 and beyond, health requires proactive care. It's easy to slip into habits that don't serve us or rely on past routines that may no longer be effective. As the years progress, our bodies undergo inevitable changes—muscle mass decreases, metabolism slows, and bones can become more brittle. However, these changes aren't reasons for giving up on health; they're invitations to adapt and redefine what it means to be healthy.

Creating a wellness routine in your 50s and beyond should focus on maintaining the balance of physical activity, nutritious eating, mental health, and self-care. The key is to keep things realistic, so you're not setting yourself up for failure with lofty goals that aren't achievable.

Real-life example:

- Linda, 58, was struggling with back pain and low energy after retiring from her teaching career. She decided to implement a morning routine that included stretching, followed by a 30-minute walk in the neighborhood. Over time, Linda noticed her energy levels rise, and her back pain significantly reduced. By setting small, realistic wellness goals, she was able to create a routine that was sustainable and aligned with her needs.

Setting S.M.A.R.T. Goals

A helpful way to structure your wellness routine is by setting S.M.A.R.T. goals (Specific, Measurable, Achievable, Relevant, and Time-bound). For example, instead of saying, "I will work out more," set a goal like, "I will walk for 30 minutes, four times a week, for the next month." This kind of goal helps you track progress, stay motivated, and make adjustments if necessary.

- Specific: Focus on clear goals (e.g., "I want to improve my flexibility").

- Measurable: Determine how to measure success (e.g., "I will track the number of steps I take each day").

- Achievable: Make sure the goal is within your capacity (e.g., "I will start with 10 minutes of stretching daily").

- Relevant: Ensure the goal aligns with your broader health vision (e.g., "Improving my flexibility will help me reduce muscle stiffness and improve my mobility").

- Time-bound: Set a timeline to assess progress (e.g., "In three months, I will be able to touch my toes while sitting").

Building Consistency Over Perfection

When creating a wellness routine, it's important to aim for consistency, not perfection. Life can get busy, and we all have setbacks, but a realistic and sustainable routine will help keep you on track. If you miss a workout or eat something indulgent, don't dwell on it. Instead, get back on track the next day.

A consistent routine doesn't mean doing everything perfectly; it means showing up for yourself consistently. Try to prioritize wellness habits every day, whether that's a short walk, drinking more water, or taking a few minutes to practice mindfulness.

Real-life example:

- George, 61, set a goal to eat healthier after his doctor recommended improving his diet. He started small by adding more vegetables to his meals and drinking more water daily. George didn't stress if he ate something unhealthy occasionally; instead, he focused on gradually improving his habits. Over time, he found himself eating fewer processed foods and feeling much better.

2. Fitness, Mobility, and Joyful Movement

The Importance of Movement in Later Life

Exercise isn't just about maintaining weight or building muscle—it's about maintaining mobility, preventing chronic conditions, and enhancing mental well-being. As we age, we lose muscle mass, bone density, and joint flexibility, but this decline can be mitigated with regular movement. The goal is not necessarily to compete in marathons but to engage in joyful movement that strengthens the body and keeps it functional.

- Strength Training: Building muscle is important for maintaining balance, posture, and joint health. Strength exercises like resistance bands, bodyweight exercises, or light weights can help increase muscle mass and prevent frailty.

- Flexibility and Mobility: Incorporating stretching or yoga into your routine helps maintain flexibility and joint health. It also helps reduce the risk of falls and injuries, which become more common with age.

- Cardiovascular Exercise: Walking, swimming, or cycling can improve heart health and endurance. Cardiovascular exercise is essential for overall health and helps increase circulation and energy levels.

Finding Joy in Movement

The most important thing about exercise after 55 is finding movement that you enjoy. When you enjoy what you're doing, it won't feel like a chore—it will become a source of joy and fulfillment.

- Explore New Activities: Try new things that excite you— whether it's dancing, hiking, swimming, or tai chi.

Experimenting with different activities allows you to discover what's fun and engaging for you.

- Walking for Mental Clarity: Walking is one of the best low-impact exercises for older adults. It improves cardiovascular health, keeps you mobile, and provides a meditative moment for reflection. Walking outside, especially in nature, has the added benefit of lifting your mood and reducing stress.

- Socialize While Exercising: Incorporating social elements into your fitness routine can help keep you motivated. Walking with a friend, joining a group yoga class, or participating in a fitness challenge are great ways to combine socializing with movement.

Real-life example:

- Linda, at 65, found herself dealing with joint pain, which made traditional exercise difficult. She turned to water aerobics and found it to be both gentle on her joints and incredibly fun. She loved the social aspect of the class and felt that the exercise improved both her physical and emotional health.

Listening to Your Body

As we age, our bodies may not respond the same way to exercise as they did when we were younger. It's essential to listen to your body and adjust your routine as needed. If something feels uncomfortable or painful, it's important to modify your activity or consult with a healthcare professional.

3. Nutrition and Vitality Over 55

The Role of Nutrition in Aging Well

Proper nutrition becomes increasingly important as we age. The body's metabolic rate slows down, and it requires fewer calories, but the quality of nutrition becomes more important than ever. To maintain vitality, we need to focus on nutrient-dense foods that support our body's changing needs.

- Protein: As we age, we need more protein to preserve muscle mass. Sources of lean protein include chicken, fish, beans, and tofu. It's also important to incorporate protein in each meal to ensure your body has a steady supply throughout the day.

- Healthy Fats: Healthy fats, such as those found in avocados, olive oil, nuts, and fatty fish (like salmon), are vital for heart health and hormone balance. Omega-3 fatty acids, in particular, are known to reduce inflammation and support brain health.

- Fiber and Whole Grains: Fiber-rich foods, such as whole grains, vegetables, and fruits, help with digestion and promote overall gut health. A high-fiber diet also helps regulate blood sugar levels, reducing the risk of diabetes.

- Antioxidants: The aging process is often associated with increased oxidative stress, which can lead to chronic diseases. Antioxidants found in fruits and vegetables, such as blueberries, spinach, and tomatoes, help reduce inflammation and protect against cellular damage.

Hydration: The Often-Overlooked Element of Nutrition

Hydration is often overlooked but is essential for maintaining overall health, especially as we age. Dehydration can lead to fatigue, dizziness, and poor digestion, among other issues. Aim to drink at least 8 cups of water a day, and more if you are physically active. Herbal teas and foods like cucumbers, watermelon, and broths can also contribute to hydration.

Eating Mindfully and Practicing Portion Control

As metabolism slows down, it's important to focus not just on what you eat but how much. Portion control and mindful eating can prevent weight gain and support better digestion. Eating slowly, paying attention to your body's hunger cues, and savoring your food are key components of mindful eating.

Real-life example:

- Tom, 66, struggled with high cholesterol and weight gain after retirement. After working with a nutritionist, he adopted a Mediterranean-style diet, focusing on whole foods and healthy fats. By tracking his meals and eating more mindfully, Tom lost weight and improved his cholesterol levels.

Conclusion: Thriving in Your Golden Years

Health is truly wealth, and in the golden years, the investment in our physical well-being pays dividends in how we feel mentally, emotionally, and socially. By embracing a realistic wellness routine that includes joyful movement, a balanced diet, and self-care, we give ourselves the best chance to thrive in our later years.

Remember, vitality doesn't come from striving for perfection; it comes from consistency, care, and understanding your body's needs. As we continue to move, eat well, and prioritize mental health, we ensure that we don't just live longer, but that we live well—fully engaged and connected to the world around us. It's not about how old we are, but about how we take care of ourselves and make the most of the years ahead. The foundation of true vitality is built on making informed choices and creating a wellness routine that works with your body, not against it.

CHAPTER 12

DOWNSIZING, RELOCATING, OR NESTING IN

~~❦~~

Introduction: The Emotional Landscape of Space

As we move through different stages of life, our relationship with the spaces we inhabit evolves. In later years, many people find themselves making significant decisions about where they live and how much space they need. These decisions often come with a mix of emotional and practical considerations, especially for those who have spent decades in one home or accumulated a lifetime's worth of possessions. Whether it's downsizing to a smaller home, relocating to a new area, or staying put and renovating to suit a new lifestyle, these choices are deeply intertwined with our sense of identity, comfort, and future planning.

This chapter will explore the process of making peace with space and stuff, the lifestyle decisions involved in relocation versus renovation, and how to create a home that genuinely reflects your evolving life in your golden years. We'll delve into the emotions of letting go of possessions, how to navigate the physical and emotional complexities of downsizing, and offer practical tips for creating a living environment that supports your mental well-being and the life you want to lead.

1. Making Peace with Space and Stuff

Letting Go of the Past: The Emotional Challenge of Downsizing

For many, the process of downsizing is more than just about reducing the number of physical belongings; it's about making peace with the memories attached to those things. Over the years, we accumulate items that represent important moments in our lives: family heirlooms, photos, furniture, and keepsakes. These belongings carry sentimental value, and the idea of parting with them can evoke feelings of loss and nostalgia.

The key to downsizing successfully lies in reframing the emotional attachment to these items. Letting go doesn't mean you're forgetting the memories they represent; it means choosing to honor those memories without being burdened by the objects. Emotional attachment can be one of the most challenging aspects of downsizing, but it can also be an opportunity for self-reflection and personal growth.

The Decision to Let Go: Practical Tips for Downsizing

1. Start Small: Don't attempt to declutter everything in one go. Begin with one room or even a small section of a room, such as a closet or drawer. Break down the task into manageable chunks to prevent feeling overwhelmed.

2. Categorize Your Belongings: Create categories for your possessions: things you absolutely need, things that have sentimental value, things you rarely use, and things that you can easily part with. This will help you decide what stays and what goes.

3. The "One-Year Rule": If you haven't used an item in the past year, it may be time to let it go. This simple rule helps you

assess what truly serves you and what is just taking up space.

4. Cherish Memories in a New Way: For sentimental items that you can't bear to part with, consider digitizing photos or videos to preserve the memories without the physical clutter. You can also make a keepsake box for the most precious items that will be easy to store.

5. Ask for Help: Downsizing can be an emotional experience, and it's okay to ask for help. Whether it's a professional organizer, a friend, or a family member, having support during this process can ease the emotional burden.

Real-life Example:

- Marie, a 62-year-old retiree, had lived in the same house for over 30 years. When it came time to move, she realized she was holding on to furniture and items from her children's childhoods. Though it was difficult, Marie began by tackling one room at a time, starting with the attic. By slowly going through her belongings and asking herself if she truly needed each item, Marie was able to part with many things. She kept a few sentimental items, like old family photos, and decided to donate the rest. By the end of the process, she felt lighter and more liberated, knowing that her memories were preserved in a new, manageable way.

2. Relocation vs. Renovation: Lifestyle Decisions

When to Relocate

For some, the idea of moving to a new area—whether it's closer to family, to a sunnier climate, or simply to downsize— becomes an appealing option. Relocation can offer the chance for a fresh start, the opportunity to live in a more convenient area, or to live in a place that better suits your physical and emotional needs. However, moving is a big decision that requires careful consideration.

- Closeness to Family and Friends: For many, being closer to loved ones is a motivating factor for relocation. This could mean moving closer to children or grandchildren or finding a community that offers social support.

- Climate and Environment: Some people seek a change of scenery in retirement, whether that means moving to a more temperate climate or a location with outdoor activities like hiking, swimming, or fishing. If your current environment is contributing to stress or poor health, a change of scenery could have a positive impact on your well-being.

- Financial Considerations: Relocation may offer an opportunity to live in a more affordable area, particularly if you move from an expensive city to a more rural location. Alternatively, relocating could provide the chance to reduce housing costs if you downsize.

When to Renovate

For others, the idea of staying in their current home is more appealing. Renovating or making modifications to your home can provide a comfortable and cost-effective way to adjust your living space to suit your new needs. A home renovation is particularly attractive if you've lived in your current home for many years and have strong emotional ties to it.

- Aging in Place: One of the most common reasons people opt for renovations is to age in place. With thoughtful home modifications, such as wider doorways, no-step entries, or grab bars in bathrooms, your home can be made more accessible as you age. Aging in place allows you to stay in a familiar environment while adapting it to meet your evolving physical needs.

- Customizing for Comfort: Home renovations give you the opportunity to reimagine your living space to better reflect your current lifestyle. Whether you want to create a home office, add a library, or design a garden space, renovations offer the freedom to make your home truly your own.

- Cost Considerations: While relocating can be expensive— due to moving costs, agent fees, and the potential for higher property prices—renovations may be a more affordable option, especially if you only need minor adjustments to your living space.

Real-life Example:

- Steven, 63, had been living in his suburban home for over 35 years. As his health began to decline, he realized that climbing stairs and maintaining a large garden were becoming increasingly difficult. After weighing his options, he decided to stay and renovate his home to accommodate his needs. He converted the basement into a ground-level suite, added a wheelchair ramp, and renovated the kitchen to make it more accessible. The renovation allowed Steven to remain in the home he loved while ensuring it would continue to meet his needs as he aged.

3. Creating a Home That Reflects Your New Life

Finding Purpose and Meaning in Your Home

After retirement, it's essential to create a living space that reflects your evolving lifestyle and values. Whether you're downsizing, relocating, or staying in your current home, the space you inhabit should promote well-being, comfort, and joy.

Your home can be more than just a place to live—it can become a sanctuary that nurtures your mental health and emotional well-being. Consider what aspects of your current living situation bring you peace and which ones contribute to stress. Embrace the opportunity to reshape your home environment to reflect your new priorities.

- Declutter and Simplify: After a lifetime of accumulation, downsizing can feel liberating. Consider embracing a minimalist lifestyle, where you let go of excess belongings and create a space that feels open, calm, and organized.

- Create Spaces for Hobbies and Personal Interests: Think about how you can design your home to support your new interests and hobbies. Whether it's a crafting corner, a music room, or a cozy reading nook, these spaces will become a source of comfort and fulfillment.

- Focus on Comfort and Accessibility: Your home should be a place of comfort and ease. Consider factors like lighting, seating arrangements, and access to outdoor spaces to ensure that your home is both functional and aesthetically pleasing.

Reflecting Your Personal Journey

Your home should reflect the person you are today—not the person you were in your previous stages of life. Let go of outdated styles and embrace an environment that **nourishes your soul** and provides a sense of security.

- Use Colors and Textures That Bring You Joy: Color has a profound impact on mood. Consider incorporating colors that bring a sense of calm or energy, depending on the atmosphere you want to create.

- Create Meaningful Displays: Display photographs, art, and other personal mementos that reflect your journey. These items can serve as reminders of the things you value most, whether that's family, travel, or personal accomplishments.

Real-life Example:

- Dorothy, a 70-year-old retiree, felt her home had become too cluttered and outdated. After downsizing, she created a living space that reflected her love of art and nature. She repurposed old furniture, painted her walls in calming earth tones, and created a garden oasis in her backyard. This transformation brought a new sense of purpose and contentment to her home, helping her feel more at peace.

Conclusion: Creating a Space for the Future

The process of downsizing, relocating, or renovating your home is more than just about adjusting the physical space—it's about creating a place that supports your new life. As you make these decisions, remember that your home should be a reflection of who you are now, not who you were. By embracing change and letting go of the past, you can create an environment that encourages growth, connection, and comfort.

Whether you choose to stay where you are, move to a new place, or make adjustments to your existing home, the key is to align your space with your current needs and desires. Health, happiness, and peace of mind all start with your environment. Let your home be a place where you can continue to grow, evolve, and enjoy the next chapter of your life.

GIVING BACK—VOLUNTEERING AND LEGACY WORK

—◦◦❦◦◦—

Introduction: The Power of Giving Back

As we enter the later stages of life, the concept of legacy becomes more profound. For many, the question shifts from what will I leave behind? to how can I make a meaningful impact in the lives of others? Giving back, whether through volunteering, mentorship, or engaging in legacy work, offers a profound sense of fulfillment and purpose. It provides the opportunity to share your wisdom, contribute to your community, and ensure that your influence continues long after you are gone.

This chapter explores the transformative power of service and how volunteering and legacy work contribute to a sense of purpose, healing, and empowerment in our later years. We will dive into the healing and empowering effects of service, explore opportunities for mentorship, charity, and leadership, and discuss how to write your legacy or memoir to ensure that your story is preserved and passed on to future generations.

1. The Healing and Empowering Effect of Service

The Emotional and Physical Benefits of Giving Back

Volunteering and engaging in service-oriented work can be an immensely fulfilling and healing experience. Studies have shown that individuals who volunteer regularly report feeling happier, more connected to their communities, and more emotionally balanced. The act of giving doesn't just benefit others—it has profound psychological and physical effects on the giver.

- Mental Health Benefits: Serving others has been linked to improved mental health. For many people, the act of helping others gives them a sense of purpose and fulfillment. Volunteering can reduce symptoms of anxiety and depression, alleviate stress, and increase feelings of happiness and gratitude.

- Physical Health Benefits: Volunteering has been shown to contribute to improved physical health. The act of helping others, whether it's volunteering at a food bank, assisting at an animal shelter, or providing support at a hospital, often involves physical activity. This can help older adults stay physically active and engaged in their communities, which is crucial for maintaining vitality.

- Increased Social Connection: Volunteering offers opportunities to build meaningful social connections, which are vital for emotional well-being. As we age, maintaining social relationships becomes even more important, and volunteering provides a structured way to engage with others and build a sense of belonging.

Real-life example:

- Linda, a 68-year-old woman, began volunteering at her local senior center after her retirement. Not only did she make new friends, but she also felt deeply fulfilled by helping others navigate their later years. Her connection with the community gave her a new sense of purpose, and the social interactions she gained through volunteering kept her engaged and happy.

How Giving Back Leads to Personal Empowerment

One of the most empowering aspects of volunteering and service work is the way it enhances your sense of agency and control. By actively choosing to serve others, you empower yourself to make a difference. Many individuals find that helping others brings clarity to their own lives and helps them rediscover passions and strengths they might have forgotten.

- Rediscovering Purpose: Giving back helps provide a renewed sense of purpose, particularly for those who may feel they have lost direction after retiring. Whether it's mentoring a young person, helping those less fortunate, or contributing to environmental causes, service allows you to find new goals that matter to you.

- Enhancing Self-Esteem: Engaging in acts of kindness and service reinforces self-worth. When you help others, you experience a boost in confidence, which enhances your mental and emotional well-being. People who volunteer report feeling more connected to their communities and more valued.

- Leaving a Positive Mark: Volunteering allows you to leave a lasting, positive impact on your community, family, and the world. This gives you a sense of fulfillment that material possessions or personal achievements cannot match. It's about contributing something meaningful to the collective whole.

2. Opportunities for Mentorship, Charity, and Leadership

Mentorship: Sharing Your Wisdom

One of the most impactful ways to give back is through mentorship. Older adults possess a wealth of knowledge and experience, and sharing that wisdom with younger generations can be incredibly rewarding. Mentorship allows you to directly impact the personal and professional lives of others, guiding them through challenges and helping them grow into their full potential.

- Professional Mentorship: Many older adults find fulfillment in mentoring young professionals in their field of expertise. Sharing your experiences, knowledge, and advice with someone entering the workforce can help them navigate challenges, set goals, and succeed in their careers. Mentorship in the workplace not only fosters professional growth but also builds a sense of legacy and impact that extends far beyond your own career.

- Life Mentorship: Beyond the workplace, mentoring others in life skills can be equally rewarding. This could mean guiding someone through major life transitions, offering advice on relationships, or supporting them in personal development. Many individuals in their later years find it fulfilling to mentor those who are navigating difficult periods in their lives.

Real-life example:

- John, a retired lawyer, took on a mentorship role for young law students. Through regular meetings and guidance, John helped these students navigate the complex legal world, making sure they had the tools they needed to succeed. Not only did this give John a sense of purpose, but it also created a legacy of knowledge that would continue to impact future lawyers.

Charity Work: Making a Difference in Your Community

Another avenue for giving back is through **charitable work**. Many organizations rely on volunteers to carry out their missions, and older adults can play a crucial role in supporting these efforts. Charity work is an excellent way to give back to the community, whether you choose to donate your time, expertise, or resources.

- Volunteer for Causes You Care About: Whether it's supporting homeless shelters, food banks, or environmental organizations, there are countless ways to get involved in charitable work. Older adults often find that helping others in need provides deep personal satisfaction and fosters a sense of community engagement.

- Becoming a Board Member or Fundraiser: Some individuals choose to use their experience to help organizations in a more strategic capacity. Serving on a nonprofit board or helping with fundraising efforts can be a powerful way to contribute to causes you care about.

Leadership in Legacy Work: Leading by Example

As you age, you can also take on leadership roles in community-building initiatives, charitable causes, or social movements. Many people in their later years find fulfillment in leading initiatives that make a positive impact on others' lives. Whether it's organizing community outreach programs, starting an advocacy group, or establishing your own charity, leadership provides an opportunity to leave a lasting legacy.

- Passion Projects: A passion project can transform into a full-scale initiative that gives you a platform to lead others and create meaningful change. This could range from leading a youth mentoring program to creating a social enterprise that addresses a pressing social need.

3. Writing Your Legacy or Memoir

The Importance of Documenting Your Story

As you approach the later stages of life, you may feel a sense of urgency to preserve your life story. Writing a memoir or documenting your legacy ensures that your experiences, wisdom, and values are passed down to future generations. It's a way of offering your perspective, your lessons learned, and your personal history in a way that can inspire, educate, and connect with others.

- Memoirs and Storytelling: Writing a memoir doesn't need to be a daunting task. It can be as simple as journaling your experiences or writing about specific periods of your life that were meaningful or transformative. Many older adults find that the process of storytelling is not only cathartic but also empowering. It allows them to reflect on their life with a sense of pride and gratitude.

- Leaving a Legacy Through Words: For those who don't wish to write a full memoir, there are other ways to leave a lasting legacy through writing. You might write letters to your children or grandchildren, reflecting on what you've learned, or offer advice for future generations. These written works can serve as gifts that are cherished for years to come.

Real-life example:

- Margaret, in her early 70s, had a career in teaching and had traveled the world. After retirement, she decided to write her memoir, reflecting on her professional journey, her travels, and the lessons she learned along the way. Margaret's memoir became a treasured family heirloom, and it also served as a source of inspiration for younger women in her community.

Conclusion: The Legacy of Service

Giving back is not just about what you do for others, but also about what it does for you. Whether through mentorship, charity, or legacy work, the act of giving is one of the most fulfilling ways to spend your later years. Service allows you to stay connected, purposeful, and fulfilled, ensuring that your life continues to have meaning and impact long after retirement.

Building a legacy—whether through acts of kindness, community service, or storytelling—is a powerful way to ensure that your wisdom, values, and experiences live on. By embracing the opportunity to serve others, you create a ripple effect that extends far beyond your own life. And in doing so, you leave a legacy that reflects the depth of your character, the richness of your experiences, and the compassion you've shown to others.

CHAPTER 14

TECH-SAVVY, FEAR-FREE—EMBRACING THE DIGITAL WORLD

∾◦❦◦∾

Introduction: The Digital Shift in Later Life

As technology continues to evolve, so does the way we live, work, and connect with others. While some may view technology as intimidating or complicated, it has become an essential tool for staying connected, engaged, and empowered, especially in later life. The idea that digital tools and platforms are only for younger generations is quickly being debunked, and more older adults are embracing technology to enrich their daily lives. The digital age offers an opportunity to stay connected with loved ones, pursue new business ventures, and engage in lifelong learning, all from the comfort of home.

In this chapter, we'll explore how to embrace technology in your golden years by mastering the basics, staying connected through social media and virtual communities, and discovering online opportunities for business, education, and personal growth. Whether you're new to digital tools or simply looking to enhance your existing skills, this chapter will provide practical tips and real-life examples of how technology can bring joy, convenience, and empowerment to your life.

1. Mastering the Basics of Tech (Safely!)

Understanding the Digital World

The first step to becoming comfortable with technology is understanding the basics. Many older adults may feel overwhelmed by terms like Wi-Fi, apps, or cloud storage. However, these concepts are easy to grasp once broken down into smaller pieces. Think of technology as a tool that can make your life easier, whether that's staying in touch with family, managing finances, or finding new hobbies.

- Computers and Tablets: At the core of modern technology are devices like computers, laptops, and tablets. These devices enable you to access the internet, communicate with others, and explore countless digital services. If you're just starting out, consider taking a basic class at your local community center, library, or online to get acquainted with operating a device.

- Smartphones: Smartphones are powerful tools that combine a phone, camera, and computer into one small device. Many older adults have found smartphones to be extremely helpful for staying connected with family, managing tasks, and accessing the internet. With simple touch-screen navigation and intuitive apps, smartphones are increasingly accessible and easy to use.

- The Internet: The internet is a vast network of information, entertainment, and connection. The first step to navigating it is understanding the basic components: search engines, websites, and online platforms. Popular search engines like Google help you find information quickly, while websites offer news, shopping, and entertainment. With just a few clicks, you can access an almost unlimited amount of knowledge and resources.

Learning Basic Skills

To build a strong foundation, focus on learning the following basic digital skills:

1. Navigating the Internet: Understanding how to use a search engine like Google to find information is key. Practice typing questions into the search bar, browsing websites, and reading articles.

2. Using Email: Email remains one of the most common forms of communication. Learn how to set up an email account, send messages, attach files, and organize emails into folders.

3. Online Security: One of the most important aspects of using technology is ensuring that your devices and personal information are safe. Familiarize yourself with basic security measures, such as using strong passwords, enabling two-factor authentication, and avoiding phishing scams. Be cautious of emails or websites asking for personal information and avoid clicking on unfamiliar links.

4. Using Apps: Apps are small software programs that can be downloaded on smartphones, tablets, and computers. Popular apps include messaging platforms like WhatsApp, social media apps like Facebook, and banking apps like Chase or PayPal. Explore the App Store or Google Play Store to download and install apps that interest you.

5. Video Calling: One of the most powerful aspects of technology is the ability to communicate with loved ones through video calling platforms such as Zoom, Skype, or FaceTime. Learning how to set up and join video calls is a

great way to stay connected with family and friends, especially if they live far away.

Real-life example:

- John, 70, had never used a computer until he decided to take an online class at his local community center. He started by learning how to send emails, browse the internet, and make video calls. Soon, he was communicating with his children and grandchildren on a regular basis, even participating in virtual family gatherings. His new skills made him feel more connected to his loved ones and gave him the confidence to explore other online activities.

2. Staying Connected Through Social Media and Virtual Communities

The Power of Social Media

Social media platforms, such as Facebook, Instagram, and Twitter, are excellent tools for staying connected with loved ones, meeting new people, and engaging with communities of shared interests. While these platforms can seem overwhelming at first, they offer incredible opportunities to connect and engage with others.

- Facebook: Facebook is one of the most popular social media platforms for older adults. It allows you to reconnect with old friends, share life updates, and engage with family members. You can join groups based on shared interests or hobbies, such as gardening, cooking, or travel, and interact with like-minded individuals. You can also use Facebook's Messenger feature for instant messaging and video calls.

- Instagram: Instagram is a photo-based platform that allows you to share pictures and videos. It's great for those who enjoy photography, travel, or simply staying updated on the lives of friends and family. Instagram is visually driven, so it can be an engaging way to see the world through the eyes of others.
- Twitter: For quick updates, news, and discussions on a variety of topics, Twitter is a great tool. You can follow your favorite brands, influencers, or public figures and join in on conversations.
- LinkedIn: For those looking to maintain a professional presence after retirement, LinkedIn is a powerful networking platform. You can stay connected with colleagues, share professional achievements, and even explore post-retirement opportunities or consulting work.

Joining Virtual Communities

Social media platforms also offer opportunities to connect with virtual communities—groups of people who share a common interest. For those over 55, joining these communities can provide support, friendship, and shared experiences.

- Online Forums: Websites like Reddit or specialized forums allow users to engage in discussions on a wide range of topics. Whether you're interested in health, hobbies, or local events, you'll find a forum for it. Many communities are welcoming to newcomers and offer a space to ask questions, share advice, and bond over shared interests.
- Virtual Support Groups: For those going through significant life transitions—such as retirement, health

issues, or grief—virtual support groups can be incredibly helpful. These groups often meet through video calls or forums and provide emotional support from others who are going through similar experiences.

- Interest-Based Online Groups: Whether you're into gardening, knitting, or travel, there's likely an online community for it. Joining a group where you can share ideas, ask questions, and make friends can be an uplifting and fulfilling way to spend your time.

Real-life example:

- Patricia, a 63-year-old woman, was feeling isolated after retiring from her job. She joined a Facebook group for women over 60 who loved gardening. Through this group, she not only learned new gardening techniques but also developed friendships with women across the country. The group became a source of support and connection, and Patricia found herself more engaged and happier.

3. Online Opportunities for Business, Learning, and Fun

Starting an Online Business After 55

Retirement doesn't have to mean stepping away from work entirely. Many older adults are turning to online business opportunities as a way to continue their careers, pursue their passions, and generate additional income. Online businesses offer flexibility, low start-up costs, and the ability to operate from anywhere.

- Freelancing: If you have expertise in a particular area, freelancing can be a rewarding opportunity. Whether it's writing, graphic design, consulting, or web development, platforms like Upwork, Fiverr, and Freelancer.com allow you to find clients and manage your own schedule.

- E-commerce: Selling products online has never been easier. Platforms like Etsy, Shopify, and Amazon allow you to set up an online shop with minimal overhead costs. If you have a craft, passion, or unique product, turning it into a business can be a fun and profitable venture.

- Teaching and Coaching: If you have a particular skill or expertise, online coaching or teaching is a great way to give back and share your knowledge. Platforms like Teachable and Udemy allow you to create courses, while Zoom can be used for live coaching sessions.

Real-life example:

- Sally, 64, decided to launch an Etsy shop after retiring from her job as a teacher. She had always enjoyed making handmade jewelry and decided to turn it into a business. Within a year, Sally's online store became successful, allowing her to continue doing something she loved while generating income.

Lifelong Learning and Personal Growth

Technology offers unlimited opportunities for learning and personal growth. Online courses and resources make it easier than ever to explore new subjects, acquire new skills, and engage in lifelong learning.

- Free and Affordable Courses: Platforms like Coursera, edX, and Skillshare offer a wealth of courses on topics ranging from technology to art to psychology. Many of these courses are free, and others offer affordable certifications that can be useful for personal growth or professional development.

- Book Clubs and Educational Groups: Many people find that joining online book clubs or educational discussion groups helps keep their minds sharp and engaged. You can participate in group reading and discussion sessions via platforms like Goodreads or Zoom.

Fun and Entertainment

In addition to learning, technology offers countless ways to stay entertained and have fun. Whether it's exploring new music, films, or online games, the possibilities are endless.

- Streaming Services: Platforms like Netflix, Amazon Prime, and Disney+ offer endless entertainment options, from classic movies to new documentaries. You can also watch educational content, such as TED Talks, to expand your knowledge.
- Online Games and Puzzles: If you enjoy puzzles, trivia, or strategy games, platforms like Lumosity and Chess.com offer interactive ways to keep your brain sharp while having fun.

Conclusion: Embracing the Digital World for a Fulfilling Future

The digital world offers countless opportunities to stay connected, learn, and thrive in retirement. By mastering the basics of technology, embracing online communities, and exploring new business ventures or hobbies, you can enrich your life and continue to grow. The key is to approach technology with curiosity and open-mindedness. It's not about being an expert but about using the tools available to enhance your life.

Whether you're reconnecting with old friends, learning a new skill, or launching a business, embracing the digital world is a powerful way to stay engaged and fulfilled. The world is at your fingertips—don't be afraid to explore, learn, and create new opportunities for yourself in this exciting digital age.

LIVING BOLDLY—WRITING YOUR NEXT CHAPTER WITH CONFIDENCE

—◦◦◦—

Introduction: Embracing the Next Chapter with Courage and Excitement

Life after retirement or in your later years is not about retreating or retiring from life—it's about embracing the next phase with confidence, purpose, and boldness. The narrative that aging means slowing down, diminishing potential, or retreating into the past is an outdated story. Instead, this chapter encourages you to celebrate what's next, while recognizing and honoring the richness of your past experiences. This chapter offers the opportunity to reshape how you think about the future, ensuring that your second act is filled with vitality, joy, and a sense of purpose.

Living boldly is about creating a life that excites you, ignites your passions, and supports your emotional, physical, and mental health. Instead of focusing on what's behind you, it's time to write your next chapter—one that is vibrant, proactive, and full of possibilities. Here, we'll explore how to embrace the future with enthusiasm, practical steps to keep your life full of energy and growth, and the "Second Bloom Challenge", a 30-day plan to kick-start your new journey.

1. Celebrating What's Next, Not Mourning What's Past

The Myth of the 'Golden Years' as the End of Excitement

The concept of retirement often brings with it the idea that life slows down after 65 or 70. For many, this period is marked by rest, relaxation, and reflection on the years gone by. While it's essential to honor the past and reflect on the accomplishments and memories that shaped you, it's equally important not to let the past define the entire trajectory of your future.

It's easy to become attached to the roles or identities you once held, whether that's in your career, as a parent, or in the hobbies that filled your earlier years. Retirement can feel like a loss of purpose, especially if you identify too strongly with a particular job or role. The truth, however, is that life is not about waiting for the next chapter; it's about actively creating it.

The first step toward living boldly is accepting that the next stage of life doesn't have to be a continuation of what was before— it can be brand new. This is the time to reframe how you look at your life: not as a conclusion, but as the start of something exciting and deeply fulfilling. Instead of focusing on what's behind, choose to celebrate and be curious about what's ahead.

Shifting from Grief to Gratitude

A key mindset shift is moving from a place of grief over what's past to one of gratitude for the experiences that have shaped you. Letting go of what no longer serves you—whether that's a career, a relationship, or even an old hobby—isn't about mourning a loss. It's about embracing the freedom to explore new possibilities, to reinvent yourself, and to design your life around the things that truly bring you joy.

As you look forward to this new phase of life, focus on the lessons you've learned, the strengths you've gained, and the joys you've experienced. The idea is to move forward with confidence—fueled by the wisdom, experiences, and resilience you've developed over the years.

Real-life Example:

- Anna, 68, recently retired after a long career as a teacher. While she initially struggled with the idea of "not working" anymore, she began to reflect on her many years in the classroom with pride. After much reflection, Anna found a new sense of excitement when she started volunteering as a tutor for adult learners, which reignited her passion for teaching and gave her a new purpose. Rather than mourning the loss of her teaching career, Anna celebrated her experience and found a way to continue contributing in a meaningful way.

2. Practical Steps to Stay Vibrant and Proactive

Creating a Life That Reflects Your Passions

As you step into your second bloom, it's important to design your days with intention. This is not about keeping busy for the sake of being busy—it's about filling your life with things that bring you joy, satisfaction, and growth. Whether it's focusing on health, pursuing a new career, or cultivating deep relationships, you have the power to create a life that is fulfilling and vibrant.

- Daily Routines that Support Your Health: Healthy habits are foundational to maintaining vitality, especially as we age. Consider integrating daily movement, a balanced diet, and mental wellness routines like journaling or mindfulness into your day-to-day life. The goal is to feel energized and centered, which will naturally propel you toward other life goals.

- Set New Goals: Retirement doesn't mean giving up on goals—it's an opportunity to create new ones. Whether it's learning a new skill, starting a creative project, or focusing on mental wellness, new goals provide direction and purpose. Break down your larger aspirations into smaller, achievable steps to maintain motivation and a sense of progress.

- Engage in Lifelong Learning: The process of learning doesn't have to stop after formal education. Whether you pursue online courses, attend workshops, or read books, engaging your mind in new ways helps keep you sharp and inquisitive.

- Build Meaningful Relationships: Focus on nurturing relationships with family, friends, and communities. Building social connections is a key factor in happiness and longevity. Invest in relationships that bring joy and contribute to your well-being.

Stay Curious and Open-Minded

The attitude of lifelong curiosity is one of the most powerful tools for maintaining vitality. Stay open to new ideas, experiences, and people. Embrace change as an exciting opportunity rather than a burden.

Real-life Example:

- James, 72, had been an accountant for over 40 years before retiring. While at first, he felt unsure about how to fill his time, he soon realized that he could start a small business based on his long-time hobby of woodworking. He joined a community of local woodworkers and began sharing his craft with others. Through his passion project, James found a renewed sense of purpose and connection with like-minded individuals.

3. The 30-Day "Second Bloom Challenge" to Launch the Journey

To kickstart this exciting new chapter, we've created the 30-Day "Second Bloom Challenge". This series of small, daily tasks is designed to help you embrace new opportunities, reflect on your goals, and take active steps toward a fulfilling future. The challenge is meant to encourage reflection, engagement, and positive habits that will set the stage for your personal renaissance.

Week 1: Reflect and Release

- Day 1: Start a gratitude journal. Write down 5 things you are grateful for today. Reflect on your life and celebrate the positive aspects.

- Day 2: Write down three things you've learned in your life that you are proud of.

- Day 3: Take 10 minutes to visualize your future—what do you want to accomplish in the next 5 years? Imagine yourself living your dream life.

- Day 4: Let go of one thing in your home or life that no longer serves you (old clothes, habits, clutter).

- Day 5: Write a letter to your future self. Reflect on where you are now and the goals you want to achieve.

Week 2: Set Your Intentions

- Day 6: Identify one new goal you'd like to achieve (learning a new skill, writing a book, taking a trip).
- Day 7: Create a vision board or digital collage that reflects your goals, dreams, and values.
- Day 8: Establish a fitness goal. This could be a daily walk, yoga, or strength training.
- Day 9: Take a 30-minute walk outside and focus on your surroundings. Reflect on how you feel and what you're grateful for.
- Day 10: Plan a trip (whether it's a weekend getaway, a cultural experience, or a relaxing retreat).

Week 3: Strengthen Your Body and Mind

- Day 11: Try a new form of exercise you've never done before (swimming, dancing, hiking).
- Day 12: Join a local learning group or club. This could be a book club, volunteer group, or educational workshop.
- Day 13: Practice mindfulness for 10 minutes. Focus on your breath, sensations, and thoughts.
- Day 14: Commit to a new hobby. Whether it's painting, knitting, or photography, give yourself permission to explore something new.
- Day 15: Declutter your workspace or an area of your home that feels chaotic or overwhelming.

Week 4: Connect and Create

- Day 16: Call or meet up with a friend you haven't spoken to in a while.
- Day 17: Set aside one hour for creative work (writing, painting, photography).

- Day 18: Explore an online course or webinar on a topic that interests you.
- Day 19: Reach out to a mentor or someone you admire and ask for advice or support.
- Day 20: Reflect on how far you've come in your 30-day challenge. Celebrate your efforts.

Conclusion: A Life of Boldness, Purpose, and Confidence

Living boldly is about embracing your life's next chapter with confidence, purpose, and a sense of adventure. Whether you're exploring new passions, starting a business, or simply discovering new ways to connect with others, your second act is an opportunity to thrive. The 30-day challenge is just the beginning. Continue to embrace change, stay curious, and pursue your goals with enthusiasm and courage.

As you enter this new phase of life, remember that strength comes from within, and confidence is built with every step you take toward creating a life that is authentically yours. Your second bloom is waiting, and it's time to bloom boldly.

LIVING BOLDLY – THE NEXT CHAPTER BEGINS

A s we have journeyed through the pages of this book, the overarching message is clear: life after 40 is not a slow decline into a passive existence, but an exciting opportunity for reinvention, growth, and fulfillment. The themes explored in these chapters—ranging from emotional wellness and mental fitness to embracing technology and legacy work—underscore the idea that the next phase of life is full of potential. It's not about "slowing down" but about living boldly, with purpose, passion, and resilience.

The process of reinvention, whether it's through discovering new hobbies, rethinking your identity, or creating a new purpose, begins with acknowledging that growth is possible at any age. We started by looking at the emotional and psychological aspects of midlife—recognizing the "invisible wall" many face around 40, and how to break through it. Through self-reflection, mindfulness, and emotional fitness, you can break free from limiting beliefs and step into a life that excites you. You are not defined by past achievements, nor are you beholden to a role that no longer serves you. Instead, you can be the architect of your own future, drawing on the wealth of wisdom, experience, and lessons learned over the years.

The discussion of mental fitness is pivotal because strong mental health forms the foundation of a successful reinvention. Strengthening the mind, understanding how stress and emotions show up differently as we age, and cultivating emotional intelligence set the stage for all other aspects of your second bloom. It's about becoming emotionally resilient, able to manage stress, and confident enough to navigate the complexities that come with midlife transitions.

The concept of redefining masculinity explored in Chapter 4 is equally crucial. It acknowledges the need for men to let go of outdated ideals, such as the tough guy persona, and embrace vulnerability. Recognizing that strength in vulnerability is not a weakness but a source of power is a transformative shift. It allows men to approach relationships, leadership, and self-awareness with authenticity and depth, laying the groundwork for richer emotional connections and personal growth.

We also delved into physical health, understanding that fitness is not just about maintaining a youthful appearance but about functioning well—staying mobile, healthy, and energetic. Whether it's adopting a wellness routine, focusing on nutrition, or practicing mindful movement, physical health plays an integral role in the aging process. The brain-body connection reinforces the idea that taking care of your body leads to mental clarity and better overall well-being, making it easier to face the challenges that come with aging.

The exploration of relationships—how they change over time and how to nurture new and existing connections—underscores the importance of social engagement. As we grow older, friendships and community become crucial pillars of well-being. Building a circle of support and staying socially active ensures that you continue to thrive emotionally and mentally. The shift in focus from individualistic pursuits to community-based goals enables you to leave behind a legacy of connection and shared wisdom.

The chapter on entrepreneurship after 55 speaks to the growing trend of older adults embracing the entrepreneurial spirit. Retirement is no longer an automatic gateway to "resting" but a call to innovate and create. Whether launching a business, mentoring, or pursuing a passion project, older adults are realizing that the skills, expertise, and knowledge accumulated over a lifetime make them well-positioned to succeed in business ventures or social entrepreneurship.

Equally important is the recognition that learning doesn't stop after retirement. The chapter on lifelong learning stresses that the desire to expand your mind and acquire new skills is a lifelong endeavor. Learning—whether through formal education, hobbies, or travel—is a critical ingredient to maintaining mental acuity and a sense of purpose. The world is full of opportunities for intellectual exploration, and embracing these opportunities helps cultivate a mindset that welcomes change, challenges, and growth.

One of the most empowering aspects of this book is the call to self-care. Emotional wellness, managing stress, and taking care of your mental health are all central to a vibrant and meaningful life. The emphasis on creating daily mental wellness routines— whether through journaling, breathwork, or simply carving out time for rest and relaxation—reminds us that our health, happiness, and longevity are in our own hands. Aging is not something to be feared; it's something to be celebrated, especially when we make self-care a priority.

Finally, as we discussed legacy and giving back, it becomes clear that the later years of life are not just about accumulating experiences, but about passing them on. Whether through mentorship, volunteering, or creating a legacy through written work, older adults have a wealth of knowledge, stories, and wisdom that can help shape the future. Legacy work allows you to create something that outlives you—be it through supporting others or through leaving behind a written or artistic testament to your journey.

In conclusion, the second bloom is about living intentionally and embracing new possibilities—whether that means taking on new challenges, reinventing your career, or deepening personal connections. The wisdom shared in this book isn't just for a select few but for anyone seeking to live a bold, vibrant, and purposeful life after 40. This stage of life is not a slowing down but an opportunity to thrive in ways that are both meaningful and fulfilling.

As you move forward in your second bloom, remember that this is your journey—a unique and personal adventure of self-discovery and growth. By taking the tools, knowledge, and insights offered in this book, you can create a future that's just as exciting and fulfilling as the life you've already lived. The second act is where your true potential lies. Embrace it with enthusiasm, confidence, and joy, knowing that your best chapters are still to come.

www.ingramcontent.com/pod-product-compliance
Lightning Source LLC
Chambersburg PA
CBHW070125030426

42335CB00016B/2270